# THE CIVIL WAR IN MARYLAND

*By*

*Daniel Carroll Toomey*

Toomey Press
Baltimore, Maryland

Also by Daniel Carroll Toomey

*A History of Relay, Maryland and the Thomas Viaduct, 1976, 1984*
*Index to the Roster of the Maryland Volunteers 1861-65, 1986*

Library of Congress Catalog Card Number 83-51066
ISBN 0-9612670-0-3

For Carol, Ruth Ann, and Danny
My Favorite Marylanders

# INTRODUCTION

The Civil War is one of the most often written about subjects in the United States. Some topics such as Robert E. Lee, Abraham Lincoln, or the Battle of Gettysburg have been covered in great detail, while others have only seen the light of day through newspaper articles, the "Official Records" or almost unattainable pamphlets published before 1920.

One topic that has received only piecemeal or superficial attention is the Civil War in Maryland. Since 1961, Harold R. Manakee's "Maryland in the Civil War", has been the only readily obtainable source for the casual reader, and a standby for the serious student of Maryland history. Its purpose was to supply a brief and impartial history in time for the Civil War Centennial.

The balance of Maryland's Civil War bibliography, for the most part, addresses single topics such as biographies, regimental histories, or the pro-Union or pro-Confederate viewpoint in a divided state; the one notable exception being the Battle of Antietam which has been covered in several excellent works.

"The Civil War in Maryland" is a chronology of military operations and major political events within the state. Its aim is two-fold: first, to dramatize the involvement and importance of Maryland, the smallest border state, during the first year of the war. Second, to recount for the first time, over 150 battles, skirmishes, and minor military operations that occurred throughout the state.

Any writer will tell you that no one person writes a book. This one is no exception. My staff consists of three very good friends, one understanding wife, and two children that doubled as cheerleaders.

My everlasting appreciation goes to Cheryl Steves who translated what no one else could have deciphered into a typed manuscript; to Erick Davis for his encouragement and contribution to accuracy; and to Bill Snavley for the unlimited use of his library and suggestions for source material. Last, but not least, a special acknowledgement to my editor, Kathleen Thomas, who made us all look good.

Daniel C. Toomey

Baltimore, Maryland
1983

# CHAPTER ONE
# 1859

As the decade of the 1850's drew to a close, it could be said that national politics had been dominated by two issues: the struggle for power in Congress between the North and the South, and the expansion of slavery into the Western Territories.

While the number of volunteer military organizations was increasing at this time, it did not represent a polarization of public opinion as much as it did an enthusiasm for military pomp and ceremony. In fact, the state of Maryland had not seen an organized military operation since the War of 1812. Therefore, the attack on Harpers Ferry in October of 1859 by John Brown had the political shock waves of a major earthquake. It significantly separated the North from the South by making the Northern Abolitionist's supposed threat on the southern way of life a reality. The combination of location and personalities involved was a terrible and accurate foretelling of the bitter Civil War that would soon engulf the country.

Although the actual attack on the United States Arsenal and attempted slave insurrection took place in Harpers Ferry, Virginia (now West Virginia), the planning and initial assualt came from the Maryland side of the Potomac River. Since this book is about Maryland, a more detailed account of that state's involvement with John Brown will be given rather than one of its sister state, Virginia.

1

However, the main story and the major events still belong to the history of Virginia.

On July 1, 1859, Brown entered the state of Maryland from Chambersburg, Pennsylvania. He used the name Isaac Smith to conceal his true identity and he covered his movements with the story that he was interested in procuring farmland near the railroad.

Brown, his sons Owen and John, and a longtime associate named Jeremiah Anderson lodged at Sandy Hook until a permanent base of operation could be found. They soon learned of a farm belonging to the Kennedy family that was available. They rented the farmhouse, cabin, and land for nine months at a one time fee of $35.00.[1] For the balance of the summer, men, supplies, and money filtered into the Kennedy farm from Abolitionists in the North.[2]

On Sunday, October 16, 1859, John Brown, the commanding general, ordered his men to secure their weapons and "proceed to the Ferry." A wagon was loaded with pikes, a sledge hammer and a crowbar. Then Brown mounted the driver's seat, donned his Kansas-worn battle cap, and headed toward the Potomac River, followed by his 18-man army of liberation. Captain Owen Brown and two men were left behind to guard the remaining supplies.[3]

At 10:30 that evening, Captain John H. Kagi and Aaron D. Stevens entered the covered bridge which carried rail and pedestrian traffic across the river between Maryland and Harpers Ferry. They captured William Williams, the night watchman, and the little army proceeded into Harpers Ferry. The United States Arsenal was occupied, and a number of prisoners were rounded up.[4]

Meanwhile, Patrick Higgins approached the covered bridge, expecting to relieve Williams as he would have on any other night. Brown's men attempted to capture him also, but Higgins fought them off and escaped into the dark to give the alarm with a bullet wound in his scalp.[5]

At 1:25 a.m., Higgins flagged down the east bound train of the Baltimore and Ohio Railroad and informed the crew of the armed men on the bridge. The engineer and baggage master went ahead on foot to investigate and were also fired upon. At the same time Hayward Sheppard, a free black employee of the railroad was shot and killed.

Brown sent word to Conductor A.J. Phelps at 3 a.m. that the train would be allowed to pass unmolested. Phelps, fearing an accident or an ambush on the bridge, awaited daybreak. As soon as there was sufficient light to see, the train raced to Monocacy Station where Phelps telegraphed William P. Smith, the master of transportation for the Baltimore and Ohio Railroad, informing him of the attack on Harpers Ferry and the death of Sheppard.[6]

Smith could not believe what he read and telegraphed back that: "Your dispatch is evidently exaggerated and written under excitement." Phelps replied from the station at Ellicott Mills, "I have not made it half as bad as it is."[7] This information was passed on to John W. Garrett, president of the railroad. Garrett in turn sent telegrams to President James Buchanan, Governor Henry Wise of Virginia, and General George Hume Stewart of the Maryland Militia, informing them an insurrection was in progress at Harpers Ferry![8]

All through the day of the 17th, Virginia Militia companies converged on Harpers Ferry and succeeded in driving Brown's men off the bridges, preventing an escape across the Potomac and Shenandoah Rivers.[9] A Martinsburg company, composed largely of railroad employees, succeeded in driving Brown out of the arsenal building and into the engine house, cutting off his last avenue of escape and releasing about 30 prisoners. At dusk, three companies arrived from Frederick, Maryland; later that night, five more arrived by train from Baltimore.[10]

President Buchanan reacted to the emergency by ordering a detachment of 90 Marines to augment the militia forces. The marines travelled by train from Washington to Relay and then west to Sandy Hook, where they were joined by Lieutenant Colonel Robert E. Lee and Lieutenant J.E.B. Stuart of the Regular Army.[11]

Lee quickly assumed command at Harpers Ferry and replaced the volunteer troops surrounding Brown's men with the Marines. Fearing accidental harm to the prisoners, Lee awaited dawn and then sent Stuart to demand Brown's surrender. Failing to talk them out, Stuart waved his cap as a signal to Lieutenant Israel Green to lead his hand-picked force of Marines in a bayonet attack on the engine house. Knocking a hole in one of the doors, they forced their way in, killing or capturing Brown and his "army."

Later in the day, Lee learned from a Maryland farmer, John Unseld, that Brown had left a stock of arms and equipment at a nearby schoolhouse. Lee ordered the Independent Greys of Baltimore, under the command of Lieutenant Colonel S.S. Miles, to secure the property. Unseld then led a detachment of Marines under Stuart to the Kennedy farm.[12] Here, they seized almost 1000 pikes, camp equipment, and a carpet bag containing 400 letters revealing Brown's plans and supporters in the North. Brown and six of his followers were hung for murder, treason and inciting slaves to insurrection. The rest of his men were killed in the two day battle.[13]

It is interesting to note how many scenes of this drama would be replayed within the next five years. Maryland and Virginia militia units would again converge on Harpers Ferry in 1861, this time to form an army for the Confederate States of America. The town of Harpers Ferry would be captured and recaptured many times during the Civil War. Lee would plan and Stuart would execute more than one attack, but on a grander scale against the same army they served in 1859. The Baltimore and Ohio Railroad would see more trains stopped, and some even stolen around the Harpers Ferry area. The railroad's president, Garrett and Master of Transportation Smith, coordinated numerous troop movements along the B&O in defense of the Union.

Thus ended 1859. 1860 would be an election year and truly the calm before the storm.

# CHAPTER TWO
# 1860

The year 1860 was not a war year for the soldiers and sailors of the United States. It was, however, the last full year of conflict between the political forces that sought to divide the nation, and those who labored to maintain the Federal Government before that issue would be determined by the sword.

Maryland's economical, geographical and political positions at this time can best be summarized by the state's present day tourism slogan, "America in Miniature." In those counties comprising the regions of Southern Maryland and the Eastern Shore, the land was flat with an abundance of rivers and creeks which served as highways for its inhabitants. The plantation was the main economic and social entity. Being isolated from the developing railroads and canals, the area reflected few changes from its colonial period. Slaves harvested tobacco crops the same as in Mississippi. Being consumers, rather than producers of manufactured goods, the landowners favored low import tariffs with the same zeal as the Georgia planters.[1]

The center of the state connected the flat, sandy plains along the Chesapeake Bay with the rugged Blue Ridge Mountains of Western Maryland. Rich farmland and water power for mills were abundant in this area of increasing elevation. Both areas were populated by a large percentage of immigrants from Ireland and Germany who represented a rapidly developing middle class society. Smaller farms utilizing free labor and producing a wider range of crops existed in lieu of the tidewater plantation. Factories and mills were erected in increasing numbers. The Baltimore and Ohio Railroad penetrated the Allegheny Mountains and connected the Port of Baltimore with the Ohio Valley, while the Philadelphia, Wilmington and Baltimore Railroad ran north from the same city.

To be certain, there were many Southern men throughout the entire state, but when the final issue came to a vote, the residents of these counties would be pro-Union and anti-slavery.[2]

Generally speaking, the institution of slavery was becoming both politically and economically unpopular. The Colonization Society of Maryland was founded by 1831 to encourage the return of free Negroes to Africa. For over 25 years, Maryland contributed $10,000 annually to the project. By 1860, almost half of the 171,000 blacks living in the state were free.[3]

Four major political parties sponsored candidates for the presidential election of 1860. Two of these held national conventions in Baltimore City.

The once strong Democratic Party met in Charleston, South Carolina in April with 606 delegates. Stephen A. Douglas was the leading candidate. The convention was disrupted when several delegations from the deep south walked out after an unfavorable vote on the issue of Popular Sovereignty. The remaining delegates agreed to adjourn the convention and to convene in Baltimore in June. The outcome of this convention was to determine the fate of the Democratic Party and the nation.[4]

The Constitutional Unionists met in Baltimore in May. Their platform simply ignored the slavery issue and emphasized preservation of the Union. John Bell of Tennessee was nominated for president. The Republicans held their convention in Chicago and nominated Abraham Lincoln of Illinois.[5]

As the second Democratic Convention convened in the Monumental City, a third convention was held in Richmond, Virginia. Here those who had left Charleston awaited the outcome of the Maryland convention before nominating a candidate. Of the eight state delegations that withdrew in Charleston, only Arkansas and Georgia actually voted in Baltimore. Senator Douglas of Illinois was nominated for president and Senator Benjamin Fitzpatrick of Alabama was nominated for vice-president.

Rejecting Douglas as a candidate, those delegates not seated at Baltimore, immediately convened their own session and nominated the vice-president of the United States, John Breckinridge for president. The Richmond assembly ratified the nomination and the Democratic Party was shattered.[6]

When Marylanders went to the polls the following November, the results were decidedly against Lincoln.

### POPULAR VOTES[7]

| | |
|---|---|
| Breckinridge | 42,497 |
| Bell | 41,177 |
| Douglas | 5,873 |
| Lincoln | 2,294 |

Despite the states three electoral votes for Breckinridge, Lincoln was elected president.[8] One final political battle remained to be fought before the shooting began. Would Maryland secede from the Union?

# CHAPTER THREE
# 1861

Thomas Holliday Hicks was governor of Maryland in 1861. Following the election of Lincoln, he was under increasing pressure by Southern sympathizers to call a special session of the state legislature to formally establish Maryland's position on state's rights. Union supporters, on the other hand, warned that such a meeting would be converted into a secession convention and petitioned against it. Mass meetings, public speeches and newspaper editorials continued to expound both causes, but Governor Hicks failed to lead the state in either direction.

On February 1, 1861, a mass meeting was held in Baltimore at the Maryland Institute Hall. A resolution was passed calling for a state convention to be held on February 15th. Other resolutions opposed any attempts by the North to force the Southern states back into the Union, and condemned Hicks for not calling the convention on his own, but did not go so far as to embrace secession.

Virginia had not yet left the Union; William Wilkins Glenn, one of the chief promoters at the meeting complained, "What astonished me most was that there were no leaders in Maryland who were willing to take a prominent part or act independently. There was but one opinion, wait for Virginia."[1]

# JANUARY 1861

**5** FORT WASHINGTON
Fearing for the safety of the nation's capitol in case of war, Secretary of the Navy, Isaac Toucey ordered a detachment of United States Marines to garrison Fort Washington on the Potomac River.

**9** FORT McHENRY
A detachment of United States Marines were sent from the Washington Naval Yard to garrison Fort McHenry.[2]

# APRIL 1861

**13** Major Robert Anderson surrendered Fort Sumter to General P.G.T. Beauregard after a 34-hour bombardment.

**15** President Lincoln issued a call for 75,000 volunteers to serve for three months to put down the insurrections.

**17** Virginia seceded from the Union.[3]

**18** BALTIMORE
Four companies of the Twenty-Fifth Pennsylvania Volunteers left Harrisburg enroute to Washington under the command of Major J.C. Pemberton. They were accompanied by two companies of U.S. Artillery bound for Fort McHenry. A member of the volunteer regiment later recalled what happened when they reached the Bolton Station. "As we disembarked from the cars we were surrounded by a hooting, yelling crowd, who lavished the most approbrious epithets upon us."
One of the companies of the Twenty-Fifth Regiment was the

Washington Artillery of Pottsville, commanded by Captain James Wren.

Wren and his men marched between two lines of Baltimore City Police officers to the waiting cars at Camden Station. Along the way, they were pelted with bricks and paving stones. Nickoles Biddle, a colored servant of Wren, was struck in the head with a paving stone. He was the first casualty of the war for the regiment.[4]

## 19-20 BALTIMORE [THE PRATT STREET RIOT]

It was on April 19, 1775, that a force of Massachusetts militia confronted the British Army at Lexington in the first battle of the American Revolution. It is ironic that the first regiment raised in response to the president's call for volunteers, the Sixth Massachusetts, would also be the first to engage in combat in the American Civil War and on the same date as their predecessors almost nine decades earlier.[5]

After reaching Philadelphia, Colonel Edward F. Jones, the commanding officer of the Sixth Massachusetts, received word that troops passing through Baltimore would be attacked by pro-Southern forces in that city. Jones ordered every gun loaded and instructed his men to ignore verbal abuse, but, if fired on, to take aim and "...be sure to drop him."[6]

At this time, rail service from the North did not connect with the southbound lines running from Baltimore to the nation's capitol. Cars were uncoupled and drawn by horses through the city to the Camden Station where they were coupled to a waiting locomotive. Upon reaching Baltimore, the first seven companies of the regiment passed through the city in this fashion without incident. Then, a large crowd formed and cut off companies C, D, I, and L, as well as the regimental band.

A cart of sand was dumped on the tracks and a number of anchors from the nearby piers were thrown across the rails. These obstructions, and the presence of a mob, caused the remaining cars to return to the President Street Station. The four companies, about 220 men, under the command of Captain A.S. Follansbee, attempted to march back along the tracks and join the rest of their regiment. They were showered with rocks, bottles and other missiles every step of the way. Finally, several pistol shots rang out. One soldier was killed, while others were wounded by stones and bullets.

The soldiers stopped their march long enough to fire a volley into the crowd, killing or wounding a number of citizens. At this point, Mayor George W. Brown placed himself at the head of the column beside Captain Follansbee in a vain attempt to stop the shooting. Finally, Marshal George P. Kane and a squad of Baltimore City Police officers formed a line in the rear of the troops, and with drawn pistols, protected the Bay Staters until they reached the safety of the train station. The regimental band and a number of Pennsylvania volunteers who were unarmed did not make the march and returned north by a special train.

Four soldiers were killed and 36 were wounded. Twelve citizens were also killed and an unknown number were wounded. [7]

It was not the size of the fight, but its location that made it significant. Maryland was on the brink of secession. The capitol was in grave danger, and Baltimore City was rapidly becoming an armed camp.

A joint communication was sent by Mayor Brown and Governor Hicks to President Lincoln, informing him that, "A collision between the citizens and the Northern troops has taken place in Baltimore and excitement is fearful. Send no troops here..." Hicks also ordered the state's military forces to aid in keeping the peace. [8]

Late that same night, word was received that a large force was headed for Baltimore from Harrisburg and Philadelphia. Lincoln had not responded to their telegram and the government officials of Baltimore City were left to confront this new threat on their own. A meeting was held between Mayor Brown and the Board of Police Commissioners. It was agreed that to avoid a second clash between soldiers and civilians, all railroad bridges north of Baltimore were to be destroyed.

A detachment of Baltimore City Police and members of the Maryland Guard were sent to burn the bridges over the Bush and Gunpowder Rivers on the Philadelphia line and three other bridges on the Northern Central Railroad. [9]

A force of about 2600 Pennsylvania volunteers came as far as Cockeysville, where they camped for a few days. At the edge of town, 400 to 500 armed civilians gathered to oppose their march. Senator Anthony Kennedy and Representative J. Morrison Harris of Maryland, in company with General Howard from Washington, travelled by coach from Baltimore to meet with the commanding officer of the Northern troops. They convinced Brigadier General George C. Wynkoop to return to Harrisburg and await further instructions, rather than fight his way into the city. When the three negotiators returned to Baltimore, they found the streets barricaded and "...guarded by armed men who swarmed in all directions."[10]

All through the day and into the night, militia companies poured into the city from surrounding counties. Confederate flags and those of the state were everywhere. The nation's flag had all but disappeared. Rumors circulated that Fort McHenry would be attacked. Five hundred thousand dollars was put at the disposal of the mayor for the defense of the city. A citizen non-uniformed corps was organized under the command of Isaac Ridgeway Trimble. Trimble later became a major general in the Confederate Army and was to lose a leg at Gettysburg.[11]

For the next two weeks, Baltimore, in the words of its mayor, assumed a position of "armed neutrality." Had Mayor Brown or Governor Hicks expounded the cause of secession, Maryland probably would have gone out of the Union. Nothing of the kind happened, however, and the issue was finally settled by a political general from Massachusetts.[12]

## 21-22    ANNAPOLIS

Brigadier General Benjamin Butler and his 800-man Eighth Massachusetts Volunteers arrived at Annapolis, Maryland aboard a ferry boat commandeered on the Susquehanna River. After conferring with Captain George S. Blake, commander of the Naval Academy, Butler ordered the Salem Zouaves to protect the training vessel *U.S.S. Constitution,* while sailors and fishermen from other companies were detailed to act as a crew. Under the command of Lieutenant George W. Rogers, the ship was taken into the Chesapeake Bay and anchored to prevent its capture.[13]

The next day, the Seventh New York arrived, and both regiments were landed. Butler led the two companies of his regiment to the railroad depot and advanced two miles out along the Annapolis and Elkridge Railroad. At the depot, they found a partially dismantled engine hidden in a shed. Butler was determined to use the engine to aid his march to Washington and asked if anyone could fix it. Private Charles Homans of Company E stepped forward and declared the engine had been built in the shop where he worked back in Massachusetts. Twenty men with railroad experience were detailed to help, and by the end of the day, the locomotive and four miles of track had been repaired.[14]

## 22 FORT CARROLL

A detachment of infantry with two pieces of artillery was sent from Fort McHenry to occupy Fort Carroll under the command of Captain J.C. Robinson, Fifth U.S. Infantry.[15]

## 23 "MARYLAND, MY MARYLAND"

James Ryder Randall was a Marylander teaching school in Louisiana. He read an account of the battle of the 19th of April, and the death of a close friend in the newspaper *Delta*. That night, he sat down and transferred his shock and grief into a nine-stanza poem entitled "My Maryland." Jennie and Hettie Cary, two sisters who lived in Baltimore, changed the title to "Maryland, My Maryland" and put it to the tune of "Lauriger Horatius," a Yale College song. Charles Ellerbrock, an employee of the printer, substituted the present tune before setting the type. It was a great favorite of the Maryland Confederate soldiers, and in 1939, it became the official state song.

## 24 ANNAPOLIS AND ELKRIDGE RAILROAD

Early on the 24th, the two Union regiments in Annapolis began a joint operation to secure the railroad as far as Annapolis Junction. From that point, they could complete their march to Washington on transportation provided by the Baltimore and Ohio line. Supporting the infantry was possibly the first rail mounted battery in military history. The tops of two cattle cars were cut off to make flat cars. A Howitzer, loaded with grape and protected by 16 riflemen, was mounted on the first car. On the second car, the gun's ammunition was stacked and guarded by six men. Next came the locomotive driven by Private Homans, and two small passenger cars, each carrying a company of infantry. About five miles out of town, this force came upon a small group of men engaged in tearing up the tracks. Seeing the train, they quickly disappeared. After repairing the damage, the first two cars were uncoupled and the soldiers attached drag lines to pull them along. This eliminated the fear of a derailment. Stopping frequently to repair the tracks, the column did not reach Millersville until 2 p.m. Here the advance guard found the bridge completely destroyed. The engineering sections went to work and by nightfall, a new bridge was built and the march continued through the night. About 4 a.m., the advance guard reached Annapolis Junction. By 10 a.m. on the 25th, the Seventh New York was boarding a special train for Washington, the first troops to reach Washington since the Pratt Street Riot. Butler remained in Annapolis, forwarding fresh troops to Washington as fast as the ships brought them, while the Eighth Massachusetts protected the railroad from future attacks.[16]

## 24 ANNAPOLIS

With the political conditions in Maryland unsettled, and the close proximity of Annapolis to the Confederacy, Federal authorities ordered the operation of the United States Naval Academy transferred to Newport, Rhode Island for the duration of the war.

On April 24, the *U.S.S. Constitution* left Annapolis Harbor in tow by the *U.S.S. R.R. Cuyler.* Aboard the *Constitution* were the midshipmen of the academy under the command of Lieutenant George W. Rodgers.[17]

## 26-MAY 14 FREDERICK CITY—SPECIAL SESSION OF THE STATE LEGIS-LATURE

On April 22, Governor Thomas H. Hicks called the Maryland State Legislature to meet in a special session at Annapolis on April 26. Hicks had long turned a deaf ear to the urging of political leaders for a special session of the legislature because he believed they would use the opportunity to pass an ordinance of secession, or in some other way, support the Southern states. After the events of April 19, he likewise feared such actions would be taken by an extra legal body of the legislature that he would be unable to control.[18]

On April 24, Governor Hicks issued orders changing the meeting place of the legislature from Annapolis to Frederick City. He did so to avoid any conflict between pro-Southern members of the legislature and General Butler's troops then occupying the state capitol. Such an occurrence would surely have mobilized political moderates behind the Southern men and greatly increased the chance of a secession movement.[19]

The legislature convened at 1 p.m. on Friday, April 26, in the courthouse at Frederick. In his message to the legislature, Governor Hicks urged moderation and avoided any strong statements in defense of the Union, or the new Confederacy.[20]

A memorial from Prince Georges County requested immediate passage of an act of secession. The Committee on Federal Relations refused to take actions on the grounds that the legislature was not empowered to take such an action. Thus, the state of Maryland was moved back a step from the brink of secession—but only a step.[21]

In the weeks that followed, several attempts were made to put the state on a war footing without aiding the South or withdrawing from the Union.

Close associations with Virginia were counter balanced by the occupation of Baltimore and Annapolis. In the end, the secession issue was fought out, or rather, talked out, in this special session of the legislature. On May 14, the special session adjourned. The same day, Governor Hicks issued a call for volunteers to fill the four regiment quotas assigned to Maryland by President Lincoln's proclamation on April 15. For the duration of his term in office, Hicks closely aligned himself with the authorities in Washington and the Union men of Maryland.[22]

## 27 DEPARTMENT OF ANNAPOLIS ESTABLISHED
Adjutant Generals Office, April 27, 1861

A new military department to be called the Department of Annapolis, headquarters at that city, will include the country for twenty miles on each side of the railroad from Annapolis to the city of Washington, as far as Bladensburg, Maryland.

Brigadier General B.F. Butler, Massachusetts Volunteers, is assigned to the command.

L. Thomas, Adjutant General[23]

# MAY 1861

The state of Maryland was kept in the Union [or, out of the Confederacy depending on the reader's point of view], by a series of bloodless campaigns during the middle months of 1861 which resulted in the seizure and occupation of strategic points by Northern troops. Without question, full credit for the seizure of Annapolis, Baltimore, and the center of the state must be given to Brigadier General Benjamin Franklin Butler. Operating at a time when events were moving too swiftly to allow the officials in Washington to formulate policy or strategy, Butler was able to transfer the opening battle lines of the Civil War from the Susquehanna to the Potomac River. Thus, the nation's capitol was spared the embarrassment of being located behind enemy lines and the Union Army did not have to fight its way through Maryland on "the road to Richmond."

**1** POTOMAC FLOTILLA ESTABLISHED
Acting on the suggestion of Commander James H. Ward, Secretary of the Navy Gideon Wells established the Potomac Flotilla for service on the Chesapeake Bay and Potomac River. Wells appointed Ward the first commander of the new naval organization.[24]

**5** RELAY
On May 3, General Winfield Scott ordered Butler to occupy the junction of the Baltimore and Ohio Railroad at Relay. At this point, the Washington Branch crossed the Patapsco River eight miles from Baltimore, while the main branch continued on to Harpers Ferry. Butler's mission was two-fold. First, stop the flow of supplies and recruits for the Confederate Army flowing from Baltimore to Harpers Ferry. Second, act as a blocking force should the enemy advance from Harpers Ferry toward that point.

On May 5, Butler occupied Relay with the Eighth New York and Sixth Massachusetts regiments and Cooks Battery. Two guns were planted on a hill to cover the bridge and a camp was established.[25]

# 10 ANNAPOLIS
Near midnight, a squad of mounted men opened fire on the pickets at Camp Butler from the opposite side of the Severn River. In all, about 20 shots were fired without anyone being hurt.[26]

# 11 ELLICOTT MILLS
At eleven o'clock in the morning, General Butler ordered the train bound from Baltimore to Ellicott Mills [now Ellicott City] seized at Relay. Two cannons and a large detachment of the Sixth Massachusetts Volunteers were loaded aboard, and the train resumed its run to the "Mills." The purpose of this movement was to intercept a steam powered artillery piece designed by Charles Dickinson and manufactured in the locomotive shop of Ross Winans. The gun was reportedly enroute to Harpers Ferry where it was to be sold to the Confederate Government.

The steam gun and the train arrived at Ellicott Mills simultaneously. The gun was quickly captured, but its inventor succeeded in escaping with some essential components which rendered the weapon inoperable. The gun was taken back to Relay where it became a great curiosity, but was never put into action. Its inventor claimed it could fire one ounce to 24-pound shot at a rate of 100 to 500 rounds per minute! Had Butler not changed the course of history, Dickinson would have, undoubtedly, been labeled the greatest gun designer or the biggest fraud of the Civil War.[27]

# 13 BALTIMORE
Having received word from Washington that Baltimore was within his department, General Butler set about to occupy the city as he had Annapolis and Relay. Five hundred men of the Sixth Massachusetts, veterans of the Pratt Street Riot, with six guns of Cooks Battery, arrived by train from Relay at dusk. Men and guns were quickly put in marching columns and occupied Federal Hill amid a thunder

storm which helped conceal their movement. The Union troops worked all night and when dawn broke, Baltimore found the American flag flying from Federal Hill and a number of well protected batteries aimed at Monument Square. Butler seized a large number of weapons destined for use against the national force and sent them to Fort McHenry for safe keeping. The next day, he issued a proclamation to the citizens of Baltimore stating the reason for the occupation, and prohibiting any actions hostile to the Federal Government. General Winfield Scott was outraged when he learned Butler had occupied Baltimore without his knowledge or approval. On the 15th he wrote, "Issue no more proclamations." Shortly thereafter, Butler was released of his command, but Baltimore remained under military control for the rest of the war.[28] General George Cadwalder became the second commander and made his headquarters at Fort McHenry.

## 13-18   RECAPTURE OF THE SMITH POINT LIGHTSHIP

On May 13, the *William Woodward* sailed from Annapolis with 100 men of the Thirteenth New York Volunteers under the command of Captain Thomas and two guns of the Eighth New York Artillery. The object of the expedition was the recapture of the Smith Point lightship which had been removed from its station by Southern sympathizers and hidden somewhere along the Great Wicomico River.[29]

The lightship was found on Mill Creek and taken in tow by the *William Woodward*. About this time, a hidden enemy opened fire from along the shoreline. The New Yorkers answered with several volleys, but were unable to bring their artillery into action. Their attackers reportedly belonged to a local militia unit known as the Lancaster Greys. Several musket balls struck the boat, but no one was injured. The expedition returned to Annapolis on May 18, having successfully completed its mission.[30]

## 14   MONOCACY BRIDGE

On the night of the 14th, a force of Southern sympathizers

attempted to disrupt the operations of the Baltimore and Ohio Railroad near the iron suspension bridge at Monocacy. Gunpowder was placed inside three culverts and exploded. The structures were damaged, but soon repaired.[31]

## 16 SEIZURE OF THE *INDIANA*

The schooner *Indiana* sailed with a cargo of nails consigned to Wheat and Brothers of Alexandria, Virginia. The vessel was seized on the night of May 16 by a boarding party from the *U.S.S. Pawnee* as it lay at anchor in the Potomac River off of Alexandria.[32]

## 19 POTOMAC RIVER OFF SEWELL'S POINT, VIRGINIA

Commander James H. Ward with his flagship the *Thomas Freeborn,* and the *U.S.S. Monticello,* commanded by Captain Henry Eagle, engaged the Confederate batteries at Sewell's Point.[33]

## 22 BALTIMORE

Ever fearful that the authorities in Baltimore City would lead the state of Maryland out of the Union, the Federal Government systematically disarmed the city and neutralized its leaders. On May 21, 1861, U.S. Marshal Washington Bonifant presented Charles Howard, president of the Baltimore City Board of Police Commissioners, with a demand for the surrender of a large number of arms owned by the city and known to be kept at the McKim house on Greenmount Avenue. The demand was backed up by 100 soldiers from Major General George Cadwalader's command.

Howard instructed Marshal Kane to escort the soldiers to the McKim house and supervise the removal of the arms to prevent any form of violence from occurring. Several wagonloads of weapons, including 400 muskets and 1500 pikes were taken to Fort McHenry.[34]

## 24 ALEXANDRIA, VIRGINIA

Commander John A. Dahlgren directed the first amphibious operation of the Civil War, resulting in the capture of Alexandria, Virginia. The expedition sailed from the Washington Naval Yard and was supported by gunboats of the Potomac Flotilla.[35]

## 24-25 THE ARREST OF JOHN MERRYMAN

At two o'clock in the morning, a detachment of Union soldiers, under orders from General William H. Keim, surrounded the home of Cockeysville farmer John Merryman. Merryman was a lieutenant in one of the volunteer companies that had been involved in burning bridges in the past month. He was arrested without a warrant and imprisoned at Fort McHenry without ever being informed of the charges against him.

The next day, Chief Justice Roger B. Taney of the Supreme Court issued a writ of *habeas corpus* and had it served on General Cadwalader, then commanding Fort McHenry. According to this document, the general was required to produce the body of John Merryman at the United States Circuit Court in Baltimore on May 27.

At the appointed hour of eleven o'clock, an aid of Cadwalader entered the courtroom and submitted a written statement to the chief justice informing him that President Lincoln had suspended the writ of *habeas corpus*. Such an action was totally unconstitutional and reveals to what extent Lincoln feared the secession movement in Maryland.

This suspension of civil liberties touched off a clash between Taney and the president of the United States. Taney, a Marylander himself, is most often remembered for his Dred Scott decision in 1857.

By the end of the year, Lincoln would totally subjudicate the state to military authority. The mayor of Baltimore, the chief of police and the police commissioner, along with 31 members of the state legislature and an assortment of congressmen, judges and newspaper editors would find accomodation in Fort McHenry as a result of their political actions.[36]

## 31-JUNE 1 POTOMAC RIVER OFF AQUIA CREEK, VIRGINIA

One of the strongest Confederate positions on the Potomac River were the batteries at Aquia Creek. Commander James H. Ward attempted to eliminate this threat to Union shipping by a concentration of naval gunfire. He shelled the Rebel position on the night of May 29 in an attempt to determine the exact location of the guns.

On the morning of June 1, Ward opened fire with the guns of the *Thomas Freeborn,* the *Anacostia* and the *Resolute.* The engagement lasted several hours until all the ships' long range ammunition was expended. One Confederate battery was silenced, but a second appeared on the high ground behind the first. Four three-inch rifled guns, under the command of Captain John S. Walker, delivered a plunging fire which could not be returned by the naval gunners. Ward pulled his ships out of range after suffering minor damage and having one man wounded.

After resupplying his guns from the newly arrived *U.S.S. Pawnee,* Ward determined to attack the Confederate batteries at Aquia Creek on the 1st of June. The *Thomas Freeborn* and the *Pawnee* engaged Rebel batteries, while the *Anacostia* and the *Reliance* remained within supporting distance.

The battle lasted for five hours and the Union ships expended over 500 rounds of ammunition. By 4 p.m., Confederate fire was reduced to a single gun. Ward broke off the engagement at this point to repair damages and rest his men. The *Freeborn* had been hit several times and was taking on water. The *Pawnee* had been hulled four times. She had also received damage to her deck and rigging, but no one was killed or seriously injured on either ship. Ward was forced to take the *Freeborn* to the Washington Naval Yard for repairs.[37]

# JUNE 1861

The Rockville Expedition was organized in early June to secure the area along the Potomac River between Washington and Harpers Ferry. It resulted in the first engagement on Maryland soil between organized forces of the Confederate States and the Union Army.

**3** FREDERICK CITY
Maryland General Assembly reconvened its special session.[38]

**8** CUMBERLAND
Colonel Lew Wallace in command of the Eleventh Regiment of Indiana Zouaves occupied Cumberland and established a camp on Rose Hill.[39]

**11** General Nathanial P. Banks assumed command of The Department of Annapolis.

**14** HARPERS FERRY
At 5 a.m., the 1000-foot long bridge that carried the Baltimore and Ohio Railroad from Maryland to Harpers Ferry was rocked by a series of explosions and fire. Within an hour, most of the structure had fallen into the Potomac River, leaving only the piers to mark its location. The work was carried out by engineers from General T.J. Jackson's Confederate force which had been occupying Harpers Ferry. The destruction of the bridge severed the main stem of the railroad.[40]

**15** SENECA MILLS
A detachment of the Second Battalion District of Columbia Volunteers skirmished with Southern forces.[41]

**17** CONRADS FERRY
Confederate forces on the opposite side of the Potomac River opened fire with a six-pound field piece on the camp of the First New Hampshire Volunteers. They expended about 20 rounds of ammunition, but caused no damage as they were apparently aiming at the flag staff and missed.

The wife of Dr. Brace was visiting the chaplain of the regiment at the time. When the firing began, she immediately mounted her horse and rode home to Poolesville where she sent a note to Captain Fletcher of the local militia company. "Virginia is firing upon

Maryland! Shall we stand idly by and let Northern men protect our homes and firesides?'' Fletcher was a Union man, but most of his company were Southern and no reinforcements were forthcoming.[42]

## 18 EDWARDS FERRY

The Confederates attempted to cross the Potomac River on a ferryboat captured from the Maryland shore. Lieutenant Henry C. Hasbrouck of Griffin's Battery, Fifth U.S. Artillery, opened fire with a 12-pound field piece, showering the boat with spherical case shot. An officer's horse jumped overboard and the attackers soon returned to the southern shore. They attempted to continue the contest with their muskets, but were soon driven off by Hasbrouck's Dragoons under Captain William T. Magruder and Companies B and G of the Seventeenth Pennsylvania Infantry.[43]

## 19 CUMBERLAND

On the morning of June 19, the Baltimore and Ohio Railroad bridge over New Creek [West Virginia] was burned by Confederate troops. The bridge was guarded by 28 men of the Cumberland Continentals under the command of Lieutenant James Clynn and Theodore Lumen. When the firing began, Captain Horace Besley hurried to the scene with a few additional men from Cumberland.

Finding the enemy force too strong to contend with, the Continentals soon retreated along the National Road back to Cumberland. This being the first military action of the war in that area, the civilian population quickly panicked. Colonel Wallace struck camp and sent his baggage to Bedford, Pennsylvania for safe keeping. Then he marched his troops a short distance out of town to await the Rebel attack. The Zouaves were soon joined by the Continentals, the Union Home Guard and militia from as far away as Frostburg and Wellersburg. By the end of the day it became evident the Confederates were not going to attack the town and everyone returned to their normal duties.[44]

## 24 WILLIAMSPORT
Confederate pickets exchanged shots across the river with Federal troops. A battery of 24-pounders, manned by gunners who had been at Fort Sumter and commanded by Captain Abner Doubleday, drove them off after firing about eight rounds.[45]

## 27 BALTIMORE
Union troops, by order of General Winfield Scott, arrested Marshal George P. Kane of the Baltimore City Police Department. The same day, Colonel John R. Kenly, First Maryland Volunteers was put in charge of the police department and the police commission was abolished.[46]

## POTOMAC RIVER OFF MATHIAS POINT, VIRGINIA
The possible erection of Confederate batteries at Mathias Point was a continuous threat to traffic on the Potomac River. Tall trees and dense undergrowth in the area made it impossible for passing naval vessels to determine if batteries were actually being erected. To solve this problem, the enterprising commander of the Potomac Flotilla determined to lead a landing party of sailors onto the point to cut and burn the foliage. He would also construct his own battery there to keep the Rebels at bay.

On the morning of June 27, Commander Ward shelled Mathias Point with the guns of his flagship *Thomas Freeborn*. At 10 a.m., Ward, Lieutenant J.C. Chaplin and 34 men in boats headed for the Rebel shore. They quickly drove off a few enemy pickets and began their defoliation mission. The Confederates soon returned in greater numbers and attacked the work party. Ward ordered his men back into their boats. He returned to his ship and began shelling the Confederate infantry until they were driven off.

The work party returned to the point and began constructing sandbag fortifications and continued to hack away at the trees. At 5 p.m., Chaplin was ordered to return to the ship. His men were loading the last of their tools when they were attacked by Colonel J.M. Brockenbrough's Fortieth Virginia Infantry supported by various other commands in the area. The sailors pulled on their oars amidst a hail of lead that riddled the boats and wounded four men.

When the firing broke out, Ward went to his ship's forward gun to personally site it against the Confederate infantry. An enemy sharpshooter fired first, and Ward fell with a musket ball in the stomach. He died an hour later. His body was taken to Washington aboard the *Thomas Freeborn*. Funeral services were held in both Washington and at the Brooklyn Naval Yard to honor the first U.S. naval officer killed in the war.[47]

Despite the fact that his attempts to build a battery at Mathias Point were a failure, Ward was directly responsible for the creation of the Potomac Flotilla and contributed significantly to the defense of Washington in the early months of the war.

# 29 CAPTURE OF THE STEAMBOAT *ST. NICHOLAS*

On the afternoon of the 28th, the side-wheeler *St. Nicholas* left the port of Baltimore for Georgetown. Enroute, it stopped at Point Lookout and took on a number of passengers. These additional passengers were actually members of the Zarvona's Zouaves, a Southern military unit organized in Maryland and led by Richard Thomas. Thomas had boarded the vessel in Baltimore, disguised as a French woman carrying a considerable amount of luggage. Concealed in the trunks were his uniform and a number of weapons.

When the *St. Nicholas* had sailed a safe distance from Point Lookout, the Zouaves, armed with pistols and cutlasses, seized the ship in the name of the Confederate Government. George N. Hollins, an ex-captain in the U.S. Navy, assumed command of the ship and sailed it to a nearby Virginia port, where it was stripped of unnecessary cargo and civilian passengers.

Hollins sailed up the Rappahannock River as far as Fredericksburg, Virginia. Enroute, he captured the brig *Monticello*, 3500 bags of coffee, the schooner *Mary Pierce,* 260 tons of ice, and the *Margaret,* 270 tons of coal. When the *St. Nicholas* finally reached Fredericksburg, Governor Letcher of Virginia gave Thomas a colonel's commission in the Virginia State Army. Hollins later became an officer in the Confederate States Navy.[48]

# JULY 1861

**4** SANDY HOOK
A company of Confederate cavalry commanded by Captain John Henderson opened fire from the Virginia shore on a portion of the Ninth New York Regiment which had recently gone into camp at Sandy Hook. Two Union soldiers were killed. On the south side of the river, a civilian named Harding was wounded when he recklessly joined in the fight.[49]

**5** NANJEMOY CREEK
The *U.S.S. Dana* commanded by Acting Masters Mate Robert B. Ely captured the sloop *Teaser* in Nanjemoy Creek.[50]

**7** GREAT FALLS
Major J. Gearhard's Eighth Battalion of D.C. Volunteers were involved in a day long engagement with Confederate troops which resulted in the deaths of two men. Killed were Privates George Riggs and Martin Ohl of Company B, known as the Turner Rifles.[51] Lieutenant Anton Becker, the battalion's adjutant, requested General Joseph K.F. Mansfield send him a surgeon and reinforcements.[52]

POTOMAC RIVER
The first Confederate torpedoes [mines] were encountered by the U.S. Navy on the Potomac River.[53]

**23** The Department of Annapolis was abolished and The Department of Maryland established under the command of General John A. Dix.

# AUGUST 1861

**25** CONRADS FERRY
A Confederate battery fired approximately 80 rounds of ammunition at the ferry house, causing some damage and wounding two Federal soldiers.[54]

# SEPTEMBER 1861

**4** GREAT FALLS
At 8:30 in the morning, the Confederates opened fire across the Potomac River. They shelled the camp of the Seventh Regiment of Pennsylvania Reserves with two 24-pound Howitzers and three rifled guns. The Union artillery at Great Falls was not in a position to answer fire. Shortly thereafter, four rifled guns were brought to their support. The Rebel guns fired about 50 rounds, most of which were too high. No casualties were reported on either side.[55]

**9** RECONNAISSANCE TO SOUTHERN MARYLAND
At six o'clock in the morning, the First Massachusetts formed in a light marching order with flags flying and bands playing, moved out of Camp Union near Bladensburg. Their object was to prevent any Southern intervention with the approaching state election and to disrupt the flow of supplies and recruits known to be finding their way into the Confederacy from the region known as Southern Maryland on the lower Potomac.

That night, the soldiers bivouacked in an oak grove near Upper Marlboro, the center of government in Prince Georges County. Search parties were sent to Bristol, Smithville, and as far south as Prince Frederick in Calvert County. By engaging in friendly conversation with the local slaves, the New Englanders were able to learn the whereabouts of hidden contraband. The regiment returned to Camp Union on October 7 with nearly a wagonload of guns, swords, uniforms and one Confederate flag.[56]

## 13-17 MEMBERS OF THE MARYLAND LEGISLATURE ARRESTED

Following the Confederate victory at Bull Run in July, the Lincoln government feared now, more than ever, a secession movement in Maryland. On September 11, Secretary of War Simon Cameron issued the following order to General Nathan P. Banks, "General: The passage of any act of secession by the legislature of Maryland must be prevented. If necessary, all or any part of the members must be arrested. Exercise your own judgement as to the time and manner, but do the work efficiently."

By the 17th, Banks was able to report, "...all members of the Maryland Legislature assembled at Frederick City on the 17th instant known or suspected to be disloyal in their relations to the Government have been arrested." Also arrested were Mayor Brown, Frank Key Howard, editor of the *Baltimore Exchange,* and Thomas W. Hall, editor of the *South,* two anti-Lincoln newspapers published in Baltimore.

On September 20, Governor Hicks wrote a letter to Banks giving his stamp of approval to the political arrests. "We can no longer mince matters with these desperate people. I concur in all you have done."[57]


## 15 ANTIETAM FORD [ALSO REFERRED TO AS PRITCHARDS MILL]

Colonel John W. Geary, of the Twenty-Eighth Pennsylvania, commanded a force of infantry and artillery camped at Point of Rocks. His troops were engaged in guarding the fords along the Potomac. Learning of Confederate activity near Harpers Ferry, he sent Lieutenant Brown and seven men of the Thirteenth Massachusetts to scout the enemy. When his advance party was opposite Pritchards Mill, they were fired on from across the river. One man was killed and the rest were pinned down.

Geary sent Captain Barr, with Company L of his own regiment, to clear Loudon Heights. Major J.P. Gould, with a company and a half of the Thirteenth Massachusetts and one gun from the Ninth New York, covered the river for a mile and a half, while Geary advanced with a force of about 130 men from both regiments and one gun commanded by Lieutenant J.W. Martin, to a point known as

Maryland Ore Banks. From this sheltered position, he opened fire on the Confederates across the river. The engagement lasted about two hours.

Besides one man killed, three Union soldiers were wounded by the bursting bands of the James shells fired by their own artillery. Geary reported Confederate losses at 18 killed, 25 wounded, and Lieutenant William S. Engles of the Second Virginia Volunteers captured. He also reported the following equipment captured:[58]

> 2 12-pound iron cannons
> 2 small brass mortars
> 2 mules
> 1 wagon

## 18 BERLIN

Company A of the Twenty-Eighth Pennsylvania Infantry skirmished with a Confederate force, killing one and wounding three others.[59]

## CONRADS FERRY

At dawn, the Confederates were discovered building entrenchments on the Virginia side of the Potomac River by pickets from General Charles P. Stone's command. The Southern force was shelled by a light battery. No casualties were reported on either side.[60]

## 23 OLD TOWN

Company B of the Second Regiment Potomac Home Brigade, commanded by Captain James D. Roberts, engaged a body of cavalry belonging to the regiment of Colonel Angus McDonald. The Confederates withdrew, losing one prisoner, 10 horses and a mule.[61]

## 24 POINT OF ROCKS

Confederate scouts were observed studying the Union camp at Point of Rocks [Camp Tyndale]. Colonel John W. Geary, fearing an artillery attack from the high ground across the river, relocated his camp 250 yards to the east, where it was protected by a wooded area. The new location also proved to be an excellent site for the artillery to cover the river crossings.

At the same time, picket stations were established on Heter's and Noland's Islands to provide an early warning system for the new camp. Shortly after these new arrangements were made, a force of Confederate infantry opened fire from near the ruins of a bridge across the camp. They were soon driven off by the Union artillery. No casualties were reported on either side.[62]

## 25 POTOMAC RIVER OFF FREESTONE POINT, VIRGINIA

At the first light of day, Lieutenant E.P. McCrea, commander of the *U.S.S. Jacob Bell,* observed a work party constructing fortifications on Freestone Point. In company with the *U.S.S. Seminole,* McCrea crossed his ship to the south side of the Potomac River and shelled the point. Rebel batteries returned fire and disabled a third vessel, the *Valley City,* which was towed to safety by the *Seminole.*[63] Confederate forces in the area were under the command of Colonel Louis T. Wigfall, First Texas Infantry.[64]

### SENECA

Union pickets at the mouth of Seneca Creek detected a Confederate force on the south side of the river. A Federal battery was forced to change positions before it could get the proper range. The Rebel troops were then dispersed. The Union infantry was from LeDue's Thirty-Fourth New York Regiment.[65]

## 29 BERLIN

A section of the Ninth New York Artillery supported by Companies F and N of the Twenty-Eighth Pennsylvania Infantry, skirmished with Southern troops.[66]

### WESTMINSTER

A detachment of 42 men and a captain from Colonel Hay's

Pennsylvania Regiment took possession of 32 mini-muskets belonging to the Smallwood Infantry commanded by Captain Scott W. Roberts. The weapons and accouterments were taken to the armory of the Carroll Guards, a pro-Union company commanded by Captain George E. Wampler. The Pennsylvania soldiers spent the night in Westminster and left the next day with the captured property.[67]

# OCTOBER 1861

**4** EDWARDS FERRY
At 9 o'clock in the morning, Confederates opened fire on a Union observation post. They were driven off by the fire of three 10-pound Parrott guns.[68]

**21** ANNAPOLIS
The Port Royal Expedition sailed from Annapolis under the command of Brigadier General Thomas W. Sherman.[69]

BALLS BLUFF, VIRGINIA
During this engagement, Union forces crossed the Potomac River at Edwards Ferry, Conrads Ferry and over Harrisons Island.[70]

# NOVEMBER 1861

**3-11** EXPEDITION INTO SOUTHERN MARYLAND
On Sunday morning, November 3, the infantry brigades of General O.O. Howard and George Sykes left their camps near Washington and marched toward Lower Marlboro and Charlotte Hall respectively. Their mission was to occupy the polling places throughout Prince Georges, Calvert, Charles and Saint Marys counties and to prevent any interference with the state election to be held on November 6. During this period of time, a number of citizens were arrested, and voters in at least two precincts were obliged to take

the oath of allegiance.[71]

## 6 AUGUSTUS W. BRADFORD ELECTED GOVERNOR OF MARYLAND

Federal authorities took no chances with the gubernatorial elections of 1861. Union soldiers were evident at polling places throughout the state. Men of the Potomac Home Brigade regiments were granted three day passes so they could return home to vote. Pro-Southern voters were intimidated or arrested. It was even reported that Massachusetts soldiers voted freely in the Maryland state election. With such widespread irregularities, the outcome was never in doubt. Augustus W. Bradford, running on the Union ticket, defeated Democratic candidate, General Benjamin C. Howard for the office of governor of Maryland.[72]

## 8 MARYLAND HEIGHTS

Colonel J.W. Geary's Twenty-Eighth Pennsylvania Infantry was on alert along the Potomac River to prevent Confederates from interfering with the state elections. When a group of officers were fired on by a gun in Harpers Ferry, and a picket post opposite the Virginia Ore Bank attacked by some Rebel cavalry, Geary feared a major offense by the enemy in his sector. He sent one gun and a detachment of infantry to occupy Maryland Heights and fire into Harpers Ferry.

The only action that actually developed was the appearance of a small cavalry force which was driven off by the men stationed opposite the Ore Bank.[73]

## 10 BERLIN

An attack on the picket post of the Twenty-Eighth Pennsylvania Infantry at Berlin was driven off.[74]

## 11 POTOMAC RIVER

On November 11, 1861, the first carrier task force of the United States Navy began operations on the Potomac River. The beginning of this story goes back to August 1861, when John La-Mountain used the armed steamer *Fanny* to launch his observation balloon off Fortress Monroe in Hampton Roads, Virginia.[75]

Throughout 1861, the Potomac River represented the frontier between Union and Confederate territory. Rebel batteries controlled much of this river below Washington, and all but cut off the Northern capitol from this major supply line. Thus, the Federal Government was anxious to learn of the strength and location of these batteries through the use of observation balloons along that stretch of river.

Professor Thaddeus S.C. Lowe found the primitive conditions of roads in Southern Maryland caused great delay in the movement of his balloons and equipment by land. He therefore suggested the construction of a "balloon boat" to increase his mobility. The coal barge *George Washington Park Custis* was purchased for $150 and converted into an aircraft carrier at the Washington Naval Yard. Lacking motor power, or armaments of any kind, the barge was a ward of the Navy, but controlled by the Army.

Balloon boat and escorts sailed out of Washington on November 10, and took up position opposite Mattawoman Creek. On the 11th, Professor Lowe and General Daniel E. Sickles took off aboard the *Intrepid* to make an aerial reconnaissance of enemy positions along the lower Potomac.[76]

## 13   OCCUPATION OF ACCOMACK AND NORTHAMPTON COUNTIES, VIRGINIA

At the southern tip of Maryland's Eastern Shore are two counties belonging to the state of Virginia, Accomack and Northampton. General John A. Dix believed the residents of these counties were arming themselves, and would soon take action hostile to the National Government. He ordered Brigadier General Henry H. Lockwood to take a force of 4000 men to restore Federal authority in the area. Lockwood's command consisted of the First Eastern Shore Infantry, Captain Richard's Independent Company of Cavalry, and the Purnell Legion. This force marched across the Maryland state line on November 13 and took control of the two Confederate counties without opposition.[77]

**14** MATTAWOMAN CREEK
A schooner loaded with wood was making its way up the Potomac River, when opposite the mouth of Mattawoman Creek, the wind ceased to blow and the vessel lay dead in the water. Three Confederate guns opened fire on the stationary target from Cockpit Point. The crew quickly dropped anchor and fled to the Maryland shore.

Seeing the ship abandoned, the Confederates sent a small boarding party out, and set it on fire. As they were returned to the Virginia shore, a detachment of the First Massachusetts Infantry under Lieutenant Horatio Roberts, rowed out to the ship in a barge and extinguished the flames. Their success drew attention from the Southern battery which again opened fire on the vessel. At this time, two 10-pound Parrott rifles from Lieutenant Colonel George W. Getty's Fifth U.S. Artillery began pounding the Confederate battery and the schooner was safely brought into Mattawoman Creek.[78]


**29** SANDY HOOK
Confederate artillery shelled the camp of the Twenty-Eighth Pennsylvania. The Union troops returned fire with their long-range Enfield muskets. No casualties were reported.[79]

# DECEMBER 1861

**3** SPECIAL SESSION OF THE STATE LEGISLATURE
Newly elected Governor Augustus W. Bradford called a special session of the state legislature, "...to consider and determine the steps necessary to be taken to enable the State of Maryland to take her place with other loyal states, in defense of the Union and the Constitution."[80]


**8** DAM NUMBER 5
General T.J. Jackson's first attempts to disable the Chesapeake and Ohio Canal at Dam Number 5 were unsuccessful.

He did report the capture of one officer and seven men of the Twentieth Indiana Regiment. Two of his men were seriously wounded and one soldier was killed.[81]

**9 POTOMAC RIVER SOUTH OF FREESTONE POINT**
Lieutenant R.H. Wyman, commander of the Potomac Flotilla, observed three wagons and a number of mounted Confederate soldiers moving along a road south of Freestone Point, Virginia. He ordered the steamers *Jacob Bell* and *Anacostia* to change position and shell the wagon train, while he stood into shore with his flagship, the *Harriet Lane,* to provide counter battery fire if necessary.

The two aforementioned ships fired over 50 rounds, setting fire to a number of buildings and dispersing the wagon trains. The only Southern resistance was some harmless musket fire.[82]

**11 DAM NUMBER 4**
A detachment of the Twelfth Indiana Infantry skirmished with Southern troops under Jackson's command.[83]

**15 POTOMAC RIVER NEAR MILLSTONE LANDING**
The sloop *Victory* was engaged in running contraband through the Union blockade on the Potomac River. Pickets of the Third Indiana Cavalry spotted the sloop near Millstone Landing and gave chase. The crew abandoned ship at the first glimpse of the pursuing cavalrymen. The vessel was captured intact. Included in her cargo were 86,250 percussion caps and 87 dozen "fancy" brass buttons.[84]

**17 DAM NUMBER 5**
Confederate forces under the command of Stonewall Jackson gathered along the south bank of the Potomac River in mid-December. Jackson's plan was to damage the Chesapeake and Ohio Canal system, thus hindering the flow of supplies to Washington from the west. His command consisted of Brigadier General Richard

B. Garnett's infantry brigade, a portion of Colonel Turner Ashby's cavalry, and part of Brigadier General James H. Carson's brigade of Virginia militia.

Carson's brigade demonstrated toward Falling Waters and Williamsport, while the main forces attacked the canal at Dam Number 5. Captain R.T. Colston, Company E, Second Virginia, volunteered to command the work party because of his knowledge of the area and the dam's construction. The operation commenced on the night of December 17, however, a breach in the dam was not made until the morning of the 21st. During this time, one man was reported killed by Union troops firing from across the river.[85]

## 18 POTOMAC RIVER

At 7 a.m., Acting Master Harrison began his run down river with the U.S. steamer *Reliance* to communicate with other vessels on the lower Potomac River. By 7:30 p.m., he had successfully passed the Rebel batteries at Oppossum Nose, Shipping Point and Chapawasmic Creek. In all, 25 shots were fired at the *Reliance,* none of which took effect.[86]

## 19 FALLING WATERS

Skirmish between forces of General T.J. Jackson and Major General Nathaniel P. Banks, Union Division.[87]

POINT OF ROCKS

At 10 o'clock in the morning, the Confederates opened fire with two brass cannons from a point near Catoctin Mountain on the camp of the Twenty-Eighth Pennsylvania Infantry. The camp consisted of six companies of the regiment commanded by Lieutenant Colonel Gabriel DeKorponay, and two guns of Battery M, Pennsylvania Light Artillery. The Confederates threw about 20 rounds at the camp before Union guns responded. The first shot fired by the Yankee artillery reportedly disabled one of the brass guns.

The Confederates withdrew to the far side of the mountain, and the Union guns were moved to a point in back of the village where they shelled a force of about 150 infantry out of some old huts near the "Furnace."[88]

RUN POINT

A new Rebel battery consisting of three guns, announced its presence opposite Run Point by shelling the camp of a New Jersey regiment on the lower Potomac. One shell carried away the corner of the Clemen's house. The firing lasted until midnight.[89]

**25** FORT FREDERICK

Company H, First Maryland Infantry Regiment, skirmished with Southern troops at Fort Frederick.[90]

**31** BERLIN

Two Confederates, one dressed as a woman, attempted to draw the pickets of the Twenty-eighth Pennsylvania Infantry into an ambush. They appeared on the Virginia side of the Potomac River waving a white flag and requesting help in entering the Union lines.

Captain Pardee sent three men from Company A in a boat to pick them up. He also posted a number of riflemen in concealed positions to cover the crossing in case the "refugees" turned out to be Rebels. As the boat neared the Southern shore a group of Confederates rushed out from behind a hill and opened fire. The three men jumped overboard and shielded themselves with the boat as Pardee's riflemen provided cover fire for the return to the Maryland shore.

# CHAPTER FOUR
# 1862

There were few military operations in the state of Maryland during the first half of 1862. The primary source of combat was the Confederate batteries along the Potomac River below Washington. This threat to ships supplying the Federal capitol was unexpectedly ended in March of 1862.

General Joseph E. Johnston, the commander of all Confederate forces in Northern Virginia, feared an attack by the numerically superior Union army. In order to consolidate his strength, and at the same time be in a position to thwart the next assault on Richmond, he ordered his men to abandon their works along the Potomac and at Centreville, and to fall back to a newly prepared position on the Rappahannock River.

Shortly after the Confederates withdrew, General George B. McClellan initiated his Peninsula Campaign which moved the war from the border of Maryland to the outskirts of Richmond. At the same time, Union forces had crossed the upper Potomac and were operating in the Shenandoah Valley. Maryland's soil was free from Southern aggressors during this period of time.

The tide of war flowed back toward Maryland during the summer of 1862. General Robert E. Lee replaced the wounded General Johnston and launched a series of counter attacks which became known as the Seven Days Battles. McClellan was driven back down the peninsula and Richmond was saved. Lee reorganized his army into two corps. The First Corps was commanded by Lieutenant General James Longstreet, while command of the Second Corps was given to Lieutenant General Thomas "Stonewall" Jackson. This command structure remained unchanged until Jackson was killed at the battle of Chancellorsville in May of 1863.

Lee's army moved north to counter a new threat in the form of the Army of Virginia, led by General John Pope. Pope's army and career were destroyed at the battles of Cedar Mountain on August 9, and Second Manassas on August 27. The North was left open to invasion and the real war was about to begin in Maryland.

The shelling of camps and political arrests were all but ignored in the wake of the Antietam, Gettysburg and Monocacy campaigns. For the next three years, major Confederate offensive operations would find their beginnings and their ends in the western part of the "Free State."

# JANUARY 1862

**1** POTOMAC RIVER OFF COCKPIT POINT
The *U.S.S. Yankee* and the *U.S.S. Anacostia* began the new year by trading shots with Confederate batteries at Cockpit Point. The *Yankee* was slightly damaged during the engagement.[1]

**5** HANCOCK
Following the occupation of Bath, Virginia by a Confederate force under General T.J. Jackson, Union troops from that area retreated towards Hancock, Maryland. They were pursued by cavalry forces led by Colonel W.S.H. Baylor of Jackson's staff. Baylor dismounted his men on the outskirts of town and pushed them through the woods until halted by gunfire which killed a lieutenant and two privates. Jackson then ordered McLaughlin's battery to shell the town in retaliation of a Union bombardment of Sheperdstown, Virginia.

The next day, he sent a demand to Brigadier General F.W.

Lander, commanding the Union garrison at Hancock to surrender, or he would shell the town. Lander refused and the Confederates opened fire. At the same time, Rebel engineers began to bridge the Potomac River about two miles above the town. Learning of a relief expedition approaching from Williamsport, Jackson broke off the engagement and returned to Virginia where he soon went into winter quarters.[2]

## 8

Augustus W. Bradford was inaugurated as Governor of Maryland at the State House in Annapolis.[3]

## 9 POTOMAC RIVER OFF MARYLAND POINT

Commodore R.H. Wyman instructed the officers of the Potomac Flotilla to harass the enemy by whatever means in their power. Lieutenant Commander McGaw considered the loss of sleep an excellent example of harassment. On the night of January 8, accompanied by the *Satellite* and the *Island Bell*, he moved his ship, the *Freeborn*, to the south side of the Potomac River opposite Maryland Point. At 12:40 a.m. on the 9th, the three ships began shelling Confederate encampments at Boyd's Hole. The firing lasted until 1:30 in the morning and obviously disturbed the repose of the sleeping soldiers.[4]

## 28 SANDY HOOK

On the morning of January 28, a section of Confederate artillery, supported by cavalry, appeared in Bolivar Heights and began shelling the camp of Company B of the Twenty-Eighth Pennsylvania, which was stationed about a mile and a half above Sandy Hook. The Union soldiers returned the fire with their Enfield muskets and a section of Parrott guns.[5]

# MARCH 1862

**5** FUNDS APPROPRIATED FOR THE FAMILIES
OF THE SIXTH MASSACHUSETTS REGIMENT

The Maryland State Legislature passed a bill appropriating $7,000 "for relief of families of those belonging to the Sixth Regiment of the Massachusetts Volunteers, who were killed or disabled by wounds received in the riot on the 19th of April in Baltimore . . ."

The bill was introduced by the Honorable John V.L. Findlay and passed on March 5 after considerable debate.[6]


**7-11** THE INVASION OF DELAWARE

In early March, Colonel James Wallace of the First Eastern Shore Infantry received orders to take a portion of his regiment into Delaware to disarm a number of disloyal militia companies. Wallace and his men boarded a special train headed for Dover, Delaware. At Delmar, a station on the state line, the train stopped. Company B detrained without orders, stacked arms and refused to serve outside the state of Maryland. Wallace arrested the ringleader and ordered the remainder of Company B to return to their quarters. He then telegraphed back to Salisbury for Company C and proceeded into Delaware with the balance of his command.[7]

On the evening of the 7th, Wallace and two companies of the First Eastern Shore Regiment entered Dover, Delaware, and occupied the State House. Captain J.B. Pennington of the Haslett Guards was summoned by Colonel Wallace and ordered to turn in his weapons. When he refused, he was placed under arrest. Joseph Wise, the keeper of the State House protested to its being used to quarter troops. He was also arrested, but subsequently released.[8]

Lieutenant John E. Rastall, adjutant of the regiment, later wrote, "For three days I slept on the Speaker's platform with my saddle for a pillow." Later, Lieutenant William A. Atkins of the Guard, and John S. Pratt, clerk of the State House, were also arrested.[9]

Word quickly spread throughout Dover of the purpose of the Marylander's visit. When Wallace's men formed in front of the State House before marching to the train station, an angry crowd formed, reminiscent of the Pratt Street Riot. For an unknown reason, these troops moved to the train and left Rastall with only one company to escort the prisoners to the train. Rastall ordered his men to form a hollow square with the prisoners in the center. Then with fixed bayonets, they marched off to the train station.

The Maryland troops also went to Smyrna, New Castle and Wilmington, collecting arms and arresting persons known to be disloyal to the Union. Rastall and a detachment escorted their prisoners to Baltimore before returning to the Eastern Shore. Those men who had refused to cross the state line were discharged without honor, which kept them from receiving any veterans benefits after the war.[10]

## 9 CONFEDERATE BATTERIES ABANDONED ON THE POTOMAC RIVER

General Joseph Hooker reported all batteries between Aquia Creek and Cockpit Point destroyed by March 14, following the Confederate withdraw.[11]

## 29 THE MIDDLE DEPARTMENT ESTABLISHED

On March 29, Major General John A. Dix was appointed to command the newly created Middle Department. The states of New Jersey, Pennsylvania, Delaware, and the Eastern Shores of Maryland and Virginia belonged to this new military department. Dix, whose headquarters were in Baltimore City, was also responsible for the Maryland counties of Cecil, Harford, Baltimore and Anne Arundel.[12] Dix was very active in suppressing Southern sentiments within the state.

## 30 MAIN LINE OF THE BALTIMORE AND OHIO RAILROAD RE-OPENED

During the first half of 1862, Confederate troops under the command of Stonewall Jackson wreaked havoc with the Baltimore and Ohio Railroad. Bridges, track and whole trains were destroyed. At the same time, locomotives, cars and miles of track had been moved over land for use by Southern railroads. On March 29, railroad construction crews completed repairs to the main branch of the Baltimore and Ohio Railroad. For the first time in 10 months, trains were again running between Cumberland and Hancock.[13] A vital link to the west had been re-established for the Union war effort.

# MAY 1862

**28** ARREST OF JUDGE CARMICHAEL
On May 24, Major General John A. Dix issued orders to James L. McPhail, provost marshal of Baltimore, for the arrest of Richard B. Carmichael, a Southern sympathizer and a judge of the Circuit Court at Easton. McPhail, with a number of deputies and 125 soldiers, occupied Easton the following Tuesday. The courthouse was surrounded as McPhail entered the courtroom and told the judge he was under arrest. Two men then seized Carmichael, and a man named John L. Bishop beat him over the head with his pistol butt until Carmichael was unconscious.[14]

Carmichael was dragged from his courtroom, and taken by steamer to Fort McHenry. He was subsequently transferred to Forts Lafayette and Delaware. Six months later, he was released without ever having been charged or tried for any crime.[15]

# JUNE 1862

**1** Brigadier General John E. Wool replaced Major General John A. Dix as commander of the Middle Department.[16]

# JULY 1862

**2** President Lincoln called for 300,000 volunteers to serve for nine months.[17]

**19** Governor Bradford called for volunteers to fill the state's quota of four regiments.[18]

**28** UNION RALLY AT MONUMENT SQUARE
A mass meeting was held at Monument Square in the latter part of July. The keynote speaker was Governor A.W. Bradford who espoused the Union cause, warning of a possible draft if volunteers in sufficient numbers were not forthcoming. Also in attendance was General Wool and his staff, and the band of the Seventh New York Regiment.[19]

# AUGUST 1862

**4** President Lincoln ordered a draft to complete his call for 300,000 volunteers.[20]

# SEPTEMBER 1862

On September 2, 1862, General Robert E. Lee wrote Confederate President Jefferson Davis, "The present seems to be the most propitious times since the commencement of the war for the Confederate Army to enter Maryland."[21] Lee wanted to take the pressure off the Northern Virginia countryside and give the farmers a chance to secure the fall harvest. He also hoped to secure a considerable amount of supplies and recruits in Maryland. If not in fact, cause the state to join the Confederacy, once under the protection of his army.

The presence of a major Confederate army in Western

Maryland resulted in daily combat situations in that region throughout the month of September. Finally, the Battle of Antietam would be fought and more Johnny Rebs and Billy Yanks would die in one day than in any other single day of the war.

**3** Major General George B. McClellan is given command of the Army of the Potomac for the second time.

## EDWARDS FERRY

Listed in the Summary of Principal Events, "Official Records," Series I, Volume 19, p. 157.

**4** EDWARDS FERRY
A detachment of Company E, First Potomac Home Brigade Infantry, was attacked and driven away from the ferry.[22]

## MONOCACY AQUADUCT

On September 4, Major General Daniel Harvey Hill sent Anderson's Brigade to fire on Union supply trains at Berlin. With his two remaining brigades, he drove off Union forces at the mouth of the Monocacy River, and crossed the Potomac River at that point. That night and the next day were spent in destroying the locks and canal boats. "The aquaduct could not be destroyed for want of powder and tools," reported Hill. On the night of the 5th, General Hill moved his command to within a few miles of Frederick City.[23]

**5** POINT OF ROCKS
Company A, Fifth New York Heavy Artillery, supported by part of the Eighty-Seventh Ohio Infantry, skirmished with Confederate forces.[24]

## POOLESVILLE

Brigadier General Fitzhugh Lee led his brigade of cavalry across the Potomac River at Edwards Ferry and drove a Federal picket force out of Poolesville.

BARNESVILLE

Having secured Poolesville, Fitzhugh Lee proceeded to Barnesville where he made a camp for the night. The next day, he moved to New Market, leaving a squadron under Captain Waller to hold the town. This force was attacked and the picket post of ten men captured. Waller retreated to New Market losing one man killed and six wounded besides those captured.[25]

BERLIN

Listed in Summary of Principal Events, "Official Records," Series I, Volume 19, p. 157.

6    URBANA

Upon entering the town, the advance guard of Hampton's brigade recaptured a Confederate courier from a member of the Union signal corps. The courier had concealed the fact that he was carrying dispatches from Jefferson Davis to General Robert E. Lee.

Stuart was soon joined by Robertson's brigade, commanded by Colonel Thomas T. Munford. He remained in the area until September 12, covering the front of the Confederate Army. Fitzhugh Lee's brigade sat astride the Baltimore and Ohio Railroad in and around New Market. Hampton's brigade covered Hyattstown and Robertson's brigade protected Stuart's right flank as far as Poolesville, which was occupied by the Twelfth Virginia Cavalry.[26]

7    POINT OF ROCKS

While the Confederate Army was fording the Potomac River, Captain Charles Russell and Company I of the First Maryland Union Cavalry, made a surprise attack killing three men and capturing 17.[27]

7-8    POOLESVILLE

On the 7th, Major Robert H. Chapin of the Third Indiana Cavalry, led two squadrons of his regiment, and two from the Eighth Illinois, in a dash on Poolesville. He captured two Confederate cavalrymen and reported the town clear of the enemy.

Jeb Stuart, believing Poolesville was about to be occupied in force by the enemy, ordered Colonel Munford to stall the Union advance. Munford, acting commander of Robertson's cavalry brigade, was just entering the town when his scouts were driven in by a Union cavalry force commanded by Colonel Farnsworth of the Eighth Illinois. Farnsworth commanded his own regiment, the Third Indiana, and a section of horse artillery from the Second U.S. Artillery under Lieutenant Chapin.

As the Union advance neared the town, Munford opened fire with two guns: a Blakely and a Howitzer from Chew's Battery. The Yankee troops reformed and gave Chapin time to get his guns firing before attacking the Confederate artillery position, which was on high ground just outside of the town. Two rounds of cannister and a counter charge by the Seventh Virginia saved the Howitzer, while the Twelfth Virginia lost eight men defending the Blakely.

During this engagement, the Second Virginia under Lieutenant Colonel R.S. Burks covered the crossroads leading to Sugar Loaf Mountain. During the exchange of rifle and carbine fire, Private P.H. Bird of Company D was killed, and Sergeant J.W. Biggs of Company C was wounded.

Colonel Farnsworth reported one man killed and a dozen wounded on the Union side, with the capture of six Rebels.[28] At the end of the day, Poolesville was in the hands of Northern forces.


## 8   RECONNAISSANCE TOWARDS FREDERICK

Captain C.H. Russell captured a Rebel scout in civilian clothes. Moving on to Jefferson, he bagged the sergeant major of a Louisiana regiment. The Union advance continued to within three miles of Frederick where the Marylanders struck a Rebel picket post and drove the enemy back to within a mile and a half of Frederick.

During the retreat, the Confederates had 13 men and nine horses captured. Among the prisoners were two deserters of Company H, First Maryland Cavalry, named Wheeler and Fluharty.[29]


## MONOCACY BRIDGE

Confederate forces blew up the iron suspension bridge which carried the Baltimore and Ohio Railroad over the Monocacy River. Three spans, measuring 115 feet each, were destroyed. A water station, including the pumphouse and engine, was also burned.[30]

## 8-9 BARNESVILLE [MONOCACY CHURCH]

After occupying Poolesville, Colonel Farnsworth picketed the roads to Conrads' and Edwards' Ferries, and to Barnesville and Monocacy. The next day, he advanced the Eighth Illinois toward Barnesville, where they came upon a force of Confederate cavalry near Monocacy Church. Sending one squadron to gain the enemy's rear, the Union forces charged, capturing several prisoners and a battle flag of the Twelfth Virginia.

The Illinois regiment continued toward Barnesville until it struck Confederate pickets on the outskirts of town. These were driven through the town in a running battle which lasted for two miles. Confederate losses were reported at four killed, five wounded and 27 captured. No Union losses were reported.[31]

## 9 NOLANSVILLE

Union cavalry from the Eighth Illinois Regiment clashed with a Confederate force, losing one man wounded and killing three of the enemy.[32]

## 10 BOONSBORO

General T.J. Jackson and his staff marched from Frederick to Boonsboro and set up headquarters at the home of John Murdock, about one mile outside of town. Captain Henry Kyd Douglas and a courier, went into Boonsboro to gather information about the fords in the area and to visit some friends. They were surprised by a detachment of Union cavalry and chased out of town. Retreating, they came upon Jackson, alone, walking his horse towards town. Douglas gave a signal of danger, and the general hastily mounted his horse and made for the rear.

Just then, T.W. Latimar of the First Virginia Cavalry came along and the three men turned on the Yankees to cover Jackson's escape. Fortunately, Lieutenant A.D. Payne of the Black Horse Cavalry, who had passed through the town in advance of Douglas, heard the firing and returned at a gallop. The tables were soon turned on Captain Schaumberg and his 21 troopers. One man was killed and a number of men and horses were captured.[33]

## 10-11 SUGAR LOAF MOUNTAIN

Captain William P. Sanders with the Sixth U.S. Cavalry, supported by two guns, attempted to occupy Sugar Loaf Mountain and capture the Confederate signal station on its summit. Their advance struck the camp of the Ninth Virginia Cavalry and captured a 10-man picket post. The Confederates fell back to the base of the mountain. During the fighting, the Ninth Virginia had Lieutenant Williams of Company A killed, and Lieutenant King and four or five others of Company I were wounded.

General W.H.F. Lee and the balance of the Ninth Virginia joined Captain Waller at the eastern base of the mountain and succeeded in turning back the charging Yankee cavalry. Sanders then dismounted his troopers and renewed the attack on foot. Only Captain Knight's squadron was armed with carbines, while the entire Union force was equipped with both carbines and side arms. General Lee ordered Knight to post his men along a wooded slope, while the remainder of his command remained mounted and covered both flanks. Firing from behind logs and trees, the Southerners were able to hold their position until darkness put an end to the fighting. That night, they retreated toward Frederick.[34]

## 11 HAGERSTOWN

Lieutenant Colonel L.T. Brien's First Virginia Cavalry charged into Hagerstown and captured Lieutenant A. Nesbitt and a small number of enlisted men. For the next five days, a considerable portion of Lee's army passed through the town.[35]

## 12 FREDERICK CITY

On September 7, Major General Ambrose E. Burnside was appointed commander of the right wing of the Army of the Potomac. General McClellan ordered Burnside to move his two army corps, Hooker's Third and Reno's Ninth to Frederick City.[36] As the Union advance reached Monocacy Bridge on the National Road, it encountered the cavalry brigade of General Wade Hampton. Hampton had been detailed by Stuart to cover the rear of Lee's army as it moved westward.

Although greatly outnumbered, Hampton set about to hold off the masses of blue infantry until two detachments guarding the bridges between Frederick and Urbana could be recalled. A rifle gun was added to the two guns already in position on the turnpike, and a squadron from the Second South Carolina under Lieutenant Meighan was ordered to support the guns.

As soon as the bridge guards rejoined the main force, Hampton began to fall back towards Frederick City. Soldiers from Cox's division of the Ninth Corps pushed the retreating Confederates to the edge of town where they were stopped by a counter attack led by Captain David Waldhauer, Company F, Jeff Davis Legion and a mixed command of 24 men. They captured one gun, which had overturned on its team, and about 10 prisoners including Colonel Augustus Moor of the Twenty-Eighth Ohio. Being hard pressed by Union infantry, the gun was left on the field.[37]

Hampton retreated to Middletown and Burnside's forces marched into Frederick City.

## 13 CATOCTIN MOUNTAIN [MIDDLETOWN]

At dawn on the 13th, Colonel John F. Farnsworth led his Second Cavalry Brigade out of Frederick City along Hagerstown Pike in search of the Confederate Army. Three or four miles out, they found the Jeff Davis Legion under the command of Lieutenant Colonel W.T. Martin, and two rifled guns commanded by Captain J.F. Hart blocking a pass through the Catoctin range. Farnsworth ordered guns from Robertson's and Hain's batteries into action on the pike. Part of the Third Indiana and Eighth Illinois dismounted, formed a skirmish line and advanced against the Confederate position. Martin barricaded the road in several places and withdrew to Middletown where he turned and again opened fire on the Yankee cavalry. Union guns soon went into battery, and shelled the Rebels out of their position only to have them take up a third position behind the town. Here, a section from Gibson's Third U.S. Artillery went into action. Pushed by Farnsworth's troopers, the Confederates blew up a bridge over the Catoctin Creek and withdrew to

Turner's Gap.[38]

## 12-13 MARYLAND HEIGHTS

Having moved his army from Manassas, Virginia to Frederick City, Lee looked at the possibility of invading Pennsylvania. Before he could do so, he would have to secure his line of communications on both sides of the Potomac River. Unfortunately for him, the Union garrisons at Harpers Ferry and Martinsburg had made no effort to escape. Now 12,000 to 15,000 Yankees lay between the Army of Northern Virginia and its supply base at Winchester. To move north without first neutralizing this threat invited disaster.

On September 9, 1862, Lee issued Special Order #191, instructing Jackson to encircle Harpers Ferry from three directions; capture or drive the garrison at Martinsburg in on the main force; and effect the surrender of Harpers Ferry. Longstreet was to move his command north as far as Boonsboro and wait for Jackson to catch up. A copy of this same order was found by Private Barton W. Mitchell of the Twenty-Seventh Indiana, when his regiment stopped for a rest in Frederick on the morning of September 12. Thus, McClellan received the "lost dispatch" and learned of the scattered condition of Lee's army just west of South Mountain.[39]

Although Harpers Ferry was in Virginia, [now West Virginia], the high ground running along the north shore of the Potomac known as Maryland Heights, was one of the key defensive positions of the town. Once occupied, no Yankee in town could hide from the plunging fire of the enemy cannons on the heights.

Lee ordered Major General Lafayette McLaws to take his and General Anderson's divisions across South Mountain and move against Maryland Heights via Pleasant Valley. McLaws passed through the mountains at Brownsville Gap on the 11th and camped about six miles from his target that night. The next day, he sent Kershaw's and Barksdale's brigades to Solomon's Gap, with orders to attack the Union left flank and drive it the length of the heights. Other Confederate units surrounded the base of Maryland Heights sealing off any means of escape from Harpers Ferry.[40]

The Union forces on Maryland Heights were commanded by Colonel Thomas H. Ford of the Thirty-Second Ohio. Ford's command on the 11th consisted of his own regiment, a squadron of

Rhode Island Cavalry under Major Augustus W. Corliss, three companies of the First Regiment Potomac Home Brigade led by Major John A. Steiner, Company H and I of the First Maryland Cavalry, and Company B, Fifth New York Artillery commanded by Captain Eugene McGrath. The New Yorkers served two nine-inch Columbiads and one 50-round rifled gun. A total of 1,150 men in all.

On the 12th, the Union pickets were driven in by the Confederate advance at Solomon's Gap. Ford was reinforced by a few companies of New York troops which allowed him to beef up his left flank. The Confederate attack came to a halt at about 6 p.m. when it struck a line of abatis extending across the top of the mountain between two cliffs. With darkness coming on, both sides disengaged and slept on their arms that night.

The next day, the Confederates attacked early in the morning. Breaking through the line of abatis, Barksdale's Mississippi attacked the flank and rear, while Kershaw's North Carolina brigade pressed the Union front. After about two hours of fighting, the Northern troops fell back to a line of breastworks which had been constructed a few days earlier by Captain John T. Whittier's company of the Potomac Home Brigade. At noon, Colonel Sammon arrived with seven companies of the One Hundred and Fifteenth New York Regiment. Ford sent two companies to reinforce the troops fighting at the top of the mountain, and used the other five to protect his artillery.[41] The Confederates continued to press the attack. Ford wrote Colonel Miles, "I cannot hold my men. The One Hundred and Twenty-Sixth [New York] all ran, and the Thirty-Second Ohio are out of ammunition. I must leave the hill unless you direct otherwise."[42] At 3:30 in the afternoon, Ford ordered the guns spiked and retreated to the other side of the river. By 4:30, McLaw's troops were in complete control of Maryland Heights. Cobb's brigade advanced from the valley and occupied Sandy Hook, capturing several hundred new muskets as well as other supplies.

The next day, a road was cut to the top of the heights. By 2 p.m., Captain Read and Captain Carlton had succeeded in hauling up two guns apiece from their respective batteries, and commenced shelling the Union position near Bolivar Heights.[43] Early on the morning of the 15th, Confederate batteries surrounding Harpers Ferry again opened fire. At 9 a.m., Colonel Miles called a meeting of his brigade commanders to discuss the propriety of an immediate surrender. The vote was unanimous, and by 10 a.m., the Union garrison surrendered.[44]


## 13 JEFFERSON

General Isaac P. Rodman ordered the Ninth New York to support Rush's Lancers in a reconnaissance of the road between Frederick City and Jefferson. About five miles from Frederick, they skirmished briefly with Confederate cavalry picketing the road. At this point, the balance of the First Brigade commanded by Colonel Harrison Fairchild came up and pursued the Rebels to within one or two miles of Jefferson.[45] The Confederate force was actually the Laurel Brigade commanded by Colonel Thomas Munford. Union cavalry pursued the Rebel troopers almost to Burkittsville. Here Munford ordered Colonel A.W. Harmans, Twelfth Virginia to block the road leading from Jefferson until the brigade wagon train could clear Crampton's Gap. In the running fight between the two towns, Captain T.B. Holland led his small detachment of sharpshooters in a counter attack which temporarily disrupted the Union advance. During the action, Lieutenant T.A. Tibbs was wounded and Private James P. Abbott of Company B was killed.

### BURKITTSVILLE

After fighting a rear guard action at Middletown, General Wade Hampton was ordered by Stuart to move his brigade to Burkittsville and join forces with Colonel Munford. Enroute, he found himself on a road parallel to one taken by part of the Union cavalry forces in pursuit of Munford. Hampton immediately charged with the Cobb Legion and put the blue coats to flight. Five prisoners were taken and 30 Yankees were reported killed or wounded. The Confederates lost four killed and nine wounded, including Lieutenant Colonel P.M.B. Young, who commanded the Cobb Legion.[46]


## 14 SOUTH MOUNTAIN

By the 10th of September, the only Confederate forces east of South Mountain were Stuart's three brigades of cavalry pacing the Union advance. While Lee moved with Longstreet to Hagerstown, he left the division of General Daniel Harvey Hill at

Boonsboro for the dual purpose of resisting McClellan's advance and capturing any federal troops eluding the forces encircling Harpers Ferry.

On the 13th, Stuart notified Hill that a large force of Union infantry had caused his retreat to South Mountain. Hill immediately ordered Colquitt's brigade to Turner's Gap on the National Road to support the cavalry. That night, Colquitt noticed far more campfires burning in the valley than could be accounted for by the two brigades of cavalry thought to be the only enemy in his front. He immediately sent this information to Hill who in turn passed it on to Lee.

Lee interpreted this to mean that McClellan was making a big push to save Harpers Ferry. Once across South Mountain, the Union forces would split the Army of Northern Virginia with Longstreet's command well north of the Potomac River. Lee told Hill and Stuart to defend the mountain passes and he ordered Longstreet to march to their aid.[47]

On the morning of the battle, most of Hill's 5,000 men were not even on the mountain. Colquitt's brigade was posted behind a stone wall flanking both sides of the National Road at Turner's Gap. To their right was Fox's Gap where Colonel Thomas Rosser commanded a mixed force of cavalry and the Stuart Horse Artillery. Further south was Crampton's Gap, defended by Munford's dismounted cavalry; Chew's Battery; a section of naval Howitzers belonging to the Portsmouth Battery; and two small infantry regiments belonging to Mahone's Brigade. Semmes and Mahone's brigades, of McLaw's commands, guarded Brownsville's Gap, and Hampton's brigade of cavalry picketed the area between the base of South Mountain and Point of Rocks.[48]

To assault the mountain passes, McClellan had three army corps, plus Pleasonton's Cavalry Division — in all about 30,000 men. Pleasonton commenced activities on the morning of September 14 with a reconnaissance at Turner's Gap. Dismounted cavalry, supported by Cox's infantry division, tested the willingness of the Rebels to hold the pass. As the day wore on, Reno's Ninth Corps slid to the left and zeroed in on Fox's Gap.[49]

The Confederate cavalry, now supported by Brigadier General Samuel Garland's infantry brigade, fought furiously against a numerically superior enemy. On their right, Lieutenant Colonel Rutherford B. Hayes led his Ohio Regiment to the crest of the moun-

*Colonel Robert E. Lee*

Erick F. Davis

*John Brown*

*The Kennedy farm house. John Brown used this house in Maryland as a base of operation for his attack on Harpers Ferry.*

# POSTPONED
## ADMINISTRATOR'S SALE!

By virtue of an order of the Orphans' Court of Howard County, the Subscriber, as Administrator *de bonis non* of the Estate of the late

## GEORG FOX,

Of Howard County, will sell, at the late residence of the said deceased

### ON

 WEDNESDAY, FEB. 6, 1861,

### AT TEN O'CLOCK, A. M,

The following Property of said George Fox, deceased—to wit:—

# Five Negroes!

## TWO WOMEN AND THREE BOYS.

# ☞ FARMING UTENSILS

Of various descriptions   Also, the

## HOUSEHOLD & KITCHEN

# FURNITURE!

And many articles too tedious to enumerate.

## TERMS OF SALE.

The terms of sale, as prescribed by the Court, are : all sums of $20 and under, cash; on all sums above $20 a credit of six months, the purchaser giving notes, with approved security, bearing interest from the day of sale

## WASHINGTON FOX

Feb. 6th, 1861.          ADMINISTRATOR DE BONIS NON.

F. A. HANZSCHE, Cheap Job Printer, 212 Baltimore St., near Charles St, Baltimore.

*Public notice of an estate sale. Maryland was a slave state in 1861.*

*Nick Biddle*

*Colonel Edward F. Jones*

*Marshal George P. Kane*

*Mayor George W. Brown*

Erick F. Davis

58

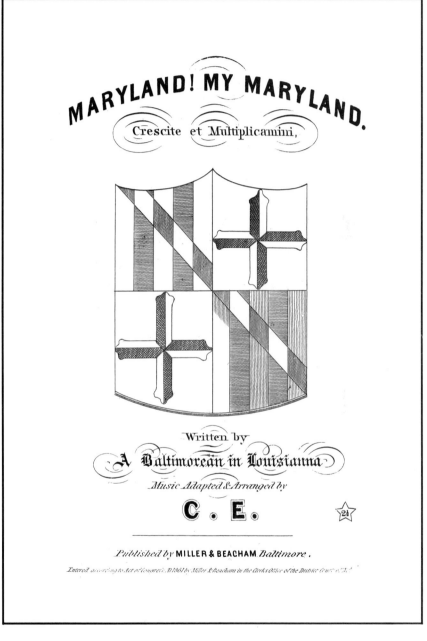

*First edition of what would become the official state song in 1939.*

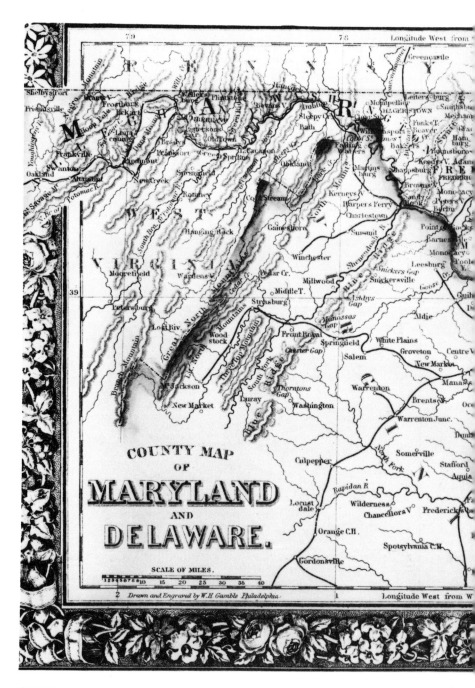

1865 Map by S. Augustus Mitchell

Maryland Hall of Records [MdHR G 1427-1167]

tain before the future president was forced to leave the field with a badly wounded arm. By 10 a.m., Garland was dead and his brigade routed. The Union troops rounded up hundreds of prisoners as they turned right and headed for Colquitt's position at Turner's Gap.[50]

Hill now paid the price for not ordering his remaining three brigades up from Boonsboro earlier. There was virtually nothing to keep the Union forces from flanking Turner's Gap. As Hill recalled, "Two guns were run down from the Mountain House and opened a brisk fire on the advancing foe. A line of dismounted staff officers, couriers, teamsters and cooks was formed behind the guns to give the appearance of battery supports. I do not remember ever to have experienced a feeling of greater loneliness." At this critical moment, the Union attack ground to a halt, while the remaining divisions of Reno's corps were brought up for the final push. During this lull in the fighting, Hill extended his right with Anderson's and Repley's brigades to fill the vacuum caused by the loss of Garland's unit. He anchored his left with General Robert Rode's brigade, and a large number of guns on a hill north of the National Road.[51]

As the vanguard of Longstreet's soldiers puffed to the end of their 13-mile forced march, McClellan ordered a general advance against the mountain passes. Both sides attacked with reinforcements as fast as they became available.

Major General Jesse Reno was personally directing the operations of the Ninth Corps near Fox's Gap when Hood's division came up to stabilize the Confederate right flank. In the twilight fighting that ensued, Reno was killed. On the left, Hooker's corps outflanked the Confederate forces by half a mile and succeeded in gaining the high ground that Rode's had fought so hard to defend.[52]

Simultaneous with the attacks at Turner's and Fox's Gaps, Major General William B. Franklin moved his Sixth Army Corps against Crampton's Gap. Here Stuart had ordered Munford to take command and "hold the post at all hazards." Munford posted his two undersized infantry regiments behind a stone wall at the base of the mountain. The cavalry were dismounted and ordered to extend both flanks, while the artillery was placed about half-way up the mountain. Two rifled guns were relocated to the top of the mountain where the added elevation improved their range.[53]

At noon, the lead brigade of the First Division, commanded by General Henry Slocom, reached Burkittsville just below Crampton's

Gap. Men from the Ninety-Sixth Pennsylvania Regiment formed a skirmish line and cleared the village of enemy pickets. Reaching the opposite end of town, they drew fire from Munford's artillery and stopped. Franklin then ordered Wolcott's First Maryland Battery to shell the enemy, while he maneuvered the First Division into position from which to launch an attack.[54]

As skirmishing developed across the side of the mountain, Munford was reinforced by 300 men from Mahone's brigade. With this small force, he held his position for three hours against the full weight of Slocom's division. Late in the afternoon, General Howell Cobb arrived with two regiments which were quickly put into position by Munford. Cobb assumed command, but before the remainder of his brigade could be put into service, the center of the Confederate line collapsed, many men being out of ammunition.

While Cobb tried in vain to rally the infantry, Munford closed the ranks of his dismounted troopers and covered their retreat. The Confederate artillery was withdrawn earlier in the day, having expended every shell in defense of the gap.[55]

The Union breakthrough was the result of a combined attack by the First Division and a brigade from General William F. Smith's command supported by the batteries of Wolcott and Ayres. Franklin reported the capture of 400 prisoners, one gun and three battle flags. Union casualties totaled 530.[56]

General McLaws reported 749 killed, wounded or missing out of a total of 1,515 engaged.[57] In a letter to Stonewall Jackson a year later, Munford remarked "the fight we had at Crampton's Gap was the heaviest I ever engaged in. . ."[58]

The Battle of South Mountain was the first major Civil War engagement in Maryland. Unfortunately, it will forever be overshadowed by the death struggle along Antietam Creek which took place just three days later. Yet the fighting was intense: both sides lost a general officer at Fox's Gap. At Crampton's Gap, Confederate losses approached 50 percent, and the outcome was significant to the course of history. Jackson was given the necessary time to complete the capture of Harpers Ferry and with it 11,000 Union soldiers, 73 cannons and 200 wagonloads of supplies and equipment desperately needed by the Confederacy.[59] Lee, though, forced to retreat that night, was given the opportunity to consolidate his army, without which, the Battle of Antietam could not have been fought.

## PETERSVILLE

A detachment of the Sixth U.S. Cavalry skirmished with Confederate forces.

## 15 BOONSBORO [ANTIETAM CREEK]

The morning following the Battle of South Mountain, Union cavalry struck the Confederate rear guard as it passed through Boonsboro. General Fitzhugh Lee and the Ninth Virginia Cavalry attempted to turn and meet the charge while being fired upon from the upper windows of some of the houses. In the melee, Lee's horse was killed. Lieutenant Colonel R.L.T. Beale of the Ninth Virginia, led a desperate counter charge that saved Lee and captured four men of the Eighth Illinois. Soon a section of Tidball's battery came up to support the National force and shelled the Rebels until the town was secured.[60]

Union losses were light. One killed and 15 wounded. General Pleasonton reported the capture of two guns and a large number of stragglers, as well as 80 dead and wounded Confederates left on the field.[61]

## GREAT WICOMICO RIVER

The *U.S.S. Thomas Freeborn*, under the command of Lieutenant Commander Samuel Magaw, captured and burned the schooner *Arctic* on the Great Wicomico River.[62]

## 16-17 ANTIETAM [SHARPSBURG]

On the night of September 14, Lee abandoned South Mountain and marched with Longstreet's corps to Sharpsburg. Here he would wait for Jackson's divisions to rejoin the army from Harpers Ferry, and for McClellan to attack. Arriving the next day, the Confederates settled in along Sharpsburg Ridge, where a combination of rock formations, low ridges and a sunken road made an excellent defensive position.

On the 16th, McClellan maneuvered Hooker's First Corps against the Confederates left flank. This resulted in some skirmishing in the afternoon and an artillery duel which lasted until after dark. Lee shifted Hood's division to the area around the Dunker Church, where the Union attack was expected on the morrow. Thus, the stage was set for the bloodiest single day of combat in American history.[63]

Lee's decision to stay and fight, rather than slip back into Virginia, was an awesome gamble. His army in the spring of 1862 had numbered 80,000.[64] Now he had less than half that number to confront McClellan's 90,000 men.[65] Furthermore, the Army of Northern Virginia was virtually irreplaceable. Its destruction might well have caused the collapse of the Confederacy, or at the very least, the fall of Richmond.

Only McClellan's generalship saved Lee. On the 17th, Northern troops attacked first, the Union right at Dunker Church, then, in the center of what became known as Bloody Lane, and finally on the right at Burnside Bridge. Had McClellan ordered a simultaneous attack along his entire front, the Confederate Army would have been destroyed. By 4 p.m., Lee had committed every regiment, and was only saved by the last minute arrival of General A.P. Hill's division which drove back the final Union advance from the very edge of Sharpsburg. Lee held his position on the 18th, but the Northern forces did not attack. That night, his army crossed over the Potomac River on pontoon bridges. By dawn, his rear guard was safely on the Virginia shore.[66]

Union and Confederate losses combined for the Battle of Antietam exceeded 23,000. Total Union losses for the Maryland Campaign including Harpers Ferry were: 26,023 killed, wounded or missing. Confederate losses for the same time period were 13,385.[67]

## 19 BLACKFORDS FORD

While Lee was concentrating his army near Sharpsburg, he left his chief of artillery, Brigadier General William N. Pendleton, to protect his line of retreat across the Potomac with the reserve artillery. Pendleton covered the river crossing at Blackfords Ford with 33 guns positioned on the Virginia shore. Eleven others were held in reserve. When the Southern forces left Maryland on the night of September 18, the survivors of Lawton's and Armistead's brigades were detailed to support the guns — about 500 men in all.[68]

Union cavalry swept the area between Sharpsburg and the Potomac on the morning of the 19th, capturing 167 stragglers, one gun and one stand of colors. When Pleasonton's troopers reached the rivers edge, Pendleton opened fire and checked their advance.[69]

The Union cavalry was soon replaced with Major General Fitz-John Porter's Fifth Corps and several batteries of artillery. Lining the river bank with riflemen and positioning his guns to take advantage of the terrain, Porter blasted away at the Confederate rear guard across the river. About 6 p.m., Union infantry forced a crossing of the river and captured four guns.[70] The rest of Pendleton's command slipped away in the darkness.

The next day, Jackson ordered Hill to return to the ford with his division and push the Union advance back across the river if possible. Hill attacked at 6:30 in the morning and caught Sykes' division about two miles inland.[71] Sykes' men and a brigade of the First Division were soon outflanked and recrossed the river to the protection of their artillery. Union losses were 92 killed, 131 wounded and 103 missing. Hill had lost 30 killed and 231 wounded.[72] The Maryland Campaign was officially over.

**20** WILLIAMSPORT
Elements of the Third Division, Sixth Army Corps skirmished with the rear guard of Lee's Army. Union losses were nine killed, 10 wounded and eight missing.[73]

**23** LINCOLN ISSUES EMANCIPATION PROCLAMATION
The proclamation declared that on January 1, 1863, "...all persons held as slaves within any state...in rebellion against the United States, shall be then, thence forward, and forever free." Since Maryland had not seceded from the Union, the Emancipation Proclamation did not apply to the slaves therein.[74]

# OCTOBER 1862

On October 8, 1862, General Robert E. Lee wrote to Jeb Stuart, "An expedition into Maryland with a detachment of cavalry if it can be successfully executed, is at this time desirable." In two days, Stuart, with 1800 men and four pieces of horse artillery, crossed

Maryland into Pennsylvania, destroyed the railroad facilities at Chambersburg, and returned safely to Virginia with several hundred captured horses and a few prisoners. From the raid, Lee learned that McClellan's army was still east of the Blue Ridge Mountains. The Keystone State was also given its first taste of war.

# 1-4 PRESIDENT LINCOLN VISITS THE ARMY OF THE POTOMAC AND MEETS WITH GENERAL GEORGE B. McCLELLAN

President Lincoln left Washington on October 1, aboard a special train provided by the Baltimore and Ohio Railroad. Accompanying the president were a few government officials and John W. Garrett, president of the Baltimore and Ohio Railroad. The train moved along the Washington branch to Relay, and then proceeded west as far as Harpers Ferry.

The president spent the next four days visiting the soldiers of the Army of the Potomac in their camps near the Antietam battlefield. He thanked the men for their efforts to preserve the Union. Then he met their commander, General George B. McClellan, in a vain attempt to get the army moving in pursuit of Lee.[75]

# 10 McCOY'S FORD

Lieutenant H.R. Phillips led 25 men of the Tenth Virginia Cavalry across the Potomac River on foot at three o'clock in the morning. They attacked a Union picket on the Maryland shore belonging to the Twelfth Illinois Cavalry. At the first sound of firing, Colonel M.C. Butler charged across the river with the balance of the regiment to secure the ford.[76]

## FAIRVIEW HEIGHTS SIGNAL STATION

First Lieutenant W.W. Rowley of the Twenty-Eighth New York Volunteers was acting signal officer at Fairview Heights. His monitoring of the Confederate operation at McCoy's Ferry was disrupted when 25 men from Hampton's brigade charged out of the morning fog and captured the signal station. Rowley and another officer escaped, and reported to Captain Russell of the First Maryland Cavalry that an enemy force estimated at four regiments and four guns was north of the Potomac.

Union losses were two privates, two horses, two sets of signal flags, two telescopes, two pairs of marine glasses and two kites. Various other items were reported lost in numbers other than two.[77]

GREEN SPRING FURNACE

At 5:30 a.m., Captain Thomas Logan of the Twelfth Illinois Cavalry was informed by a citizen named Jacques that a large Rebel force had crossed the Potomac at McCoy's Ford. Within five minutes, wagons were loaded and on the road to Clear Springs, while Logan's men formed a line of battle. Shortly thereafter, his picket force near Green Spring Furnace was driven in. Confederate cavalry quickly occupied the crossroads and planted a cannon on a hill near the furnace. Shots were exchanged for several hours before the Union cavalry fell back to Clearfield.[78]

## 12 MONOCACY RIVER

General Alfred Pleasonton moved his command to the mouth of the Monocacy River where he hoped to cut off the Confederate cavalry force before it could return to Virginia from its raid on Chambersburg. The infantry station there knew nothing of the Rebel's whereabouts. Pleasonton ordered troopers from the Eighth Illinois and the Third Indiana Cavalry, and two guns from Pennington's battery to cross the Monocacy and begin covering the fords in the direction of Poolesville. His advance soon met a body of cavalry approaching from the opposite direction. This force turned out to be Confederates wearing captured uniforms. The Rebels showed no signs of hostility until within striking distance. Then they charged the Federal troops and drove them back on their main force. More Confederate cavalry soon appeared, supported by one gun under the direction of Colonel Pelham. Pleasonton, having only a portion of his division on the field, took command of the infantry. He ordered Colonel Elijah Walker to send four companies from the Fourth Maine Regiment to support Pennington's guns, and a fifth company to aid his cavalry in repelling dismounted skirmishes.[79] At the same time, Lieutenant Colonel Moses Lakeman sent six companies of the Third Maine Infantry to support Pleasonton's men.[80]

After two hours of fighting, the Union commander learned

Stuart's cavalry was crossing the Potomac River at White's Ford, and the force in his front was screening this movement. Pleasonton immediately ordered all the infantry, except for two companies, from the mouth of the river to join his cavalry in a general advance. The balance of Pennington's battery had also come up, but the artillery horses were completely exhausted and could not move the guns near enough to shell the ford. The Confederates slowly fell back to the river and crossed at White's Ford, having successfully delayed the enemy until Stuart's entire force was safely back in Virginia.[81]

**17** First draft in Maryland during the Civil War.[82]

**18** POTOMAC RIVER OFF JACK CREEK, VIRGINIA
The *U.S.S. Jacob Bell* captured a boat operated by C.F. Waid at the mouth of Jack Creek as Waid attempted to run the blockade imposed by the Potomac Flotilla. The cargo was reportedly valued at $2,000.[83]

# NOVEMBER 1862

**1** POTOMAC RIVER OFF MARYLAND POINT
The *U.S.S. Freeborn*, commanded by Lieutenant Commander Samuel Magaw, captured three boats running the blockade at Maryland Point.[84]

**6** CHESAPEAKE BAY
The *U.S.S. Teaser*, commanded by Acting Ensign Philip Sheridan, captured the sloop *Grapshot*.[85]

**8** GLYMONT
The *U.S.S. Resolute*, under the command of Acting Master James C. Tole, captured the sloop *Capitola* at Glymont. The sloop

was running the blockade from Virginia to the Maryland shore, with both freight and passengers aboard.[86]

**9** MAJOR GENERAL GEORGE B. McCLELLAN RELIEVED OF COMMAND OF THE ARMY OF THE POTOMAC

Having failed to prod McClellan into action after their meeting in early October, President Lincoln replaced him with Major General Ambrose E. Burnside. Despite a less than spectacular performance at the Battle of Antietam, the new commander had emerged a hero of the now famous "Burnside Bridge."[87]

**16** ST. JEROME'S CREEK

The *U.S.S. T.A. Ward*, under the command of Acting Master William L. Babcock, captured the sloop *G.W. Green* and a small boat in St. Jerome's Creek. The two crafts were attempting to run the blockade with supplies for the Confederacy.[88]

**19** RELIC HUNTERS AT ANTIETAM BATTLEFIELD

On November 19, 1862, the *Baltimore Sun* ran an article about two men from York, Pennsylvania, Lieutenant Samuel Wabring and John F. Erwin. If not the first, surely the greatest Civil War relic hunters of all time. From the Antietam battlefield, adjacent camps and residents of the area, they collected the following incredible list of items: 1168 rifles, carbines and muskets; 90 gun barrels and numerous other parts; tents; entrenching tools and camp equipment; a set of ambulance springs; 26 swords; 23 boxes of bread; one box of overcoats; a box of hospital supplies; 26.5 boxes of ammunition; 8000 cartridge boxes; 14 horses and three mules! Most of the items were turned over to the Federal Quartermaster at Hagerstown. The true value of their efforts was not appreciated until a hundred years later.

**25** POOLESVILLE

Captain George W. Chiswell, a resident of Poolesville

before the war, led a detachment of White's Thirty-Fifth Virginia Battalion on a raid in his hometown. The Confederates captured two government telegraphers with all their apparatus, and about half a dozen Union soldiers who were paroled. Before returning to Virginia, Chiswell's men destroyed some supplies belonging to General George Stoneman's command and 600 muskets stored by the Philadelphia Zouaves D'Afrique.[89]

## 27 FORT WARREN, BOSTON HARBOR, MASSACHUSETTS

All Maryland political prisoners at Fort Warren were released by order of the Secretary of War, Edwin M. Stanton. They were: Severn T. Wallis, Henry M. Warfield, William G. Harris, and T. Parkin Scott, all members of the state legislature. Also released were George W. Brown, the mayor of Baltimore, Charles Howard, William Gatchell and George P. Kane of the Baltimore City Police Department, Frank Key Howard, editor of the *Baltimore Exchange*, and Thomas Hall, Jr., editor of the *South*.[90]

# DECEMBER 1862

## 14 POOLESVILLE

The Union garrison at Poolesville was enjoying a quiet Sunday with little thought of war. No pickets or guards were posted, and many of the men were attending evening services.

This same evening, Major E.V. White crossed the Potomac with a portion of his battalion and charged into Poolesville. The Union soldiers who were at the church ran toward the town hall, where they were quartered. Confederate troops opened fire, killing the orderly sergeant and wounding the rest. After a brief exchange of gunfire, the remainder of the garrison in the hall surrendered.

White killed or captured about 50 men from the Eleventh New York Cavalry, along with their horses and equipment. He also destroyed a large amount of Federal property stored there. Only one Confederate was killed, a man named Jenkins, who had taken his sick brother's place during the raid.[91]

**23** BALTIMORE
Major General Robert C. Schenck replaced General Wool as commander of the Middle Department. *The Baltimore American,* proclaimed ". . . almost any change . . . would have been hailed with acclamations."

# CHAPTER FIVE
# 1863

At the beginning of the third year of the Civil War, neither side could be assured victory. The armies and fleets of the Federal Government had attacked the Southern states on the Mississippi, in the Gulf, along the Atlantic coast and down through Northern Virginia.

Yet by January of 1863, the new Confederacy continued to repell most of these invasions and at times, engaged in offensive operations that greatly disrupted the Union war effort. Finally, the idea of European intervention on behalf of the Confederacy remained a very strong threat until the campaigns of Gettysburg and Vicksburg put the Union war machine on the road to victory in the early days of July.

# JANUARY 1863

1    THE EMANCIPATION PROCLAMATION BECAME
     LAW

All slaves held in states in rebellion against the Federal Government were forever free.[1]

**25** Major General Joseph Hooker replaces General Burnside as commander of the Army of the Potomac.

# MARCH 1863

**3** CONGRESS SUSPENDS THE WRIT OF *HABEAS CORPUS*

On March 3, 1863, the Congress of the United States gave President Lincoln the power to suspend the writ of *habeas corpus* as a special wartime measure.[2] This was almost two years after Lincoln had assumed such power in the state of Maryland with the arrest of John Merryman.

**15** PUBLICATION OF THE *ST. MARY'S BEACON* SUSPENDED

J.S. Downs, editor of the *St. Mary's Beacon,* was arrested and the newspaper was put out of business for his anti-Lincoln editorials. Downs was imprisoned at Point Lookout and later transferred to Baltimore.[3]

# APRIL 1863

**26** ALTAMONT

A detachment of the Eleventh Virginia Cavalry, led by Captain E.H. McDonald, captured the town and a stock train belonging to the Baltimore and Ohio Railroad.[4] The Confederates derailed the train by removing one of the rails and sent it crashing into the Youghiogheny River. The bridge, station and remains of the train were then set on fire.[5]

## CRANBERRY SUMMIT

Confederate cavalry under General William E. "Grumble" Jones, burned the water station and engine house on the Baltimore and Ohio Railroad. The station was garrisoned by Company D, Sixth West Virginia Infantry, of which 15 were made prisoners.[6]

## OAKLAND

General William E. Jones ordered Colonel A.W. Harman to take his Twelfth Virginia Cavalry along with the First Maryland and McNeil's Rangers to Oakland to destroy the railroad bridge.[7] The town was garrisoned by Company O of the Sixth West Virginia Infantry under the command of Captain Joseph M. Godwin. The Union soldiers were enjoying a quiet Sunday morning when a rifle shot from Private Cornelius Johnson's picket post split the air. Within minutes, Company O was gobbled up by Rebel cavalry. Two officers and 57 enlisted men were captured.

The Confederates set fire to the bridge and other railroad property. Before leaving town, they destroyed the bluecoats' muskets and paroled their prisoners.[8]

# JUNE 1863

The Gettysburg Campaign began in June as Confederate forces spilled across the Potomac River in a broad band of butternut and grey that reached from Cumberland as far east as Rockville. Lee pushed his seemingly invincible Army of Northern Virginia into Pennsylvania and lost one of the most famous military engagements in the history of the world.

During this period of time, the main line of the Baltimore and Ohio Railroad again fell into enemy hands. Service was disrupted from Sykesville to Rawlings Station, 160 miles to the west. Every important bridge between Cumberland and Harpers Ferry was destroyed. Seven miles of track were pulled up and taken south, while many more were rendered useless. The Confederates also destroyed rolling stock, station houses and maintenance shops. The resulting damage took almost two months to repair.

## 11 SENECA MILLS
On the morning of June 10, 1863, Company A, Forty-Third Battalion Partisan Rangers, was officially organized at Rector's Crossroads, Virginia. After an election of officers, Company A was joined by Captain Brawner's company, Prince Williams Cavalry. The two units, under the command of Colonel John S. Mosby, then headed toward the Potomac.

Early the next morning, Mosby sent three men across the river to capture the Union picket. The two companies then crossed the river and attacked the camp of Company I, Sixth Michigan Cavalry. The Yankees were chased out of their camp, but took up a new position around Seneca Mills. In the hand-to-hand combat near the mill, Captain Brawner and newly-elected Lieutenant George H. Whitescarver of Company A were killed.

After dispersing the Federals at the mill, Mosby returned to Seneca and destroyed their camp equipment. He then recrossed the river with 17 prisoners, 21 horses and five mules. Besides the prisoners, the Sixth Michigan unit had four killed and one wounded. Mosby reported only two killed and one wounded.[9]

## 15 WILLIAMSPORT
General A.G. Jenkins, Brigadier General of Confederate Cavalry, brushed aside Company B of Cole's Cavalry as it crossed the Potomac River at Williamsport.[10] Lieutenant Jacob A. Metz, of Company B was killed and two enlisted men were reported missing.[11]

## 17 CATOCTIN CREEK
Colonel E.V. White crossed the Potomac River below Berlin with about 165 men. Upon reaching the north shore, he divided his force. Lieutenant J.R. Crown with 62 men of Company B was sent along Frederick Road to approach Point of Rocks from behind and cut off any means of escape in that direction. White advanced along the tow path of the canal with the balance of his command to make a direct attack.

Crown and his men rode about two miles when they captured a straggler who told them he was part of two companies of Maryland cavalry on their way to Point of Rocks. Doubting the prisoner's story, Crown sent Lieutenant N.W. Dorsey and six men to secure a second prisoner. They found two men away from the main force. One was captured and the other killed.

The sound of shooting alerted the Union cavalry, which immediately crossed Catoctin Creek and formed a line of battle. The second prisoner's story was the same as the first. Crown ordered an immediate attack despite being outnumbered almost 2 to 1. Company B charged across the creek amid heavy, but inaccurate carbine fire. Closing in with pistol and saber, the Confederates soon broke the Union formation. A running battle ensued for a distance of four miles at which point, Crown broke off the action in order to secure his prisoners and aid White if needed. In all, 37 men and horses were captured.

POINT OF ROCKS

When Company B of the Thirty-Fifth Virginia Battalion reached Point of Rocks, it found that Colonel White had driven off a force of Means Independent Virginia [Union] Cavalry, capturing 20 horses and men.[12] The Confederates set fire to a train of 17 cars before returning to Virginia.[13]

CUMBERLAND

Cumberland was evacuated on the 16th following the defeat of Brigadier General Robert H. Milroy at Winchester, Virginia. The two regiments of infantry garrisoning the town and all government property was transferred to New Creek. Rolling stock and all removable property belonging to the railroad was also sent off.

On the evening of the 17th, two Confederate soldiers rode into town and presented Mayor F.A. Buckley with a written demand for the surrender of Cumberland from General John D. Imboden. A few minutes later, 350 men and two guns entered the town. The Rebels only stayed long enough to destroy the telegraph lines and some railroad property. Then gathering a number of horses from the area and a few recruits, they rode off.[14]

## 20 MIDDLETOWN

A Union signal party was driven from the outskirts of town by Confederate cavalry.

## 21 FREDERICK

At 6 a.m., four Union cavalrymen were pursued down the Hagerstown Road and into the city by 20 men from Gilmor's Second Maryland Cavalry led by Captain T. Sturgis Davis. Three of the Yankees were captured just east of town. The fourth, an officer, made good his escape.[15]

Later the same day, the tables turned as Captain George Vernon and 40 men of Company A, Cole's Cavalry, chased Gilmor's men out of Frederick, killing one, wounding one and capturing three others.[16]

### MOUNT AIRY

Telegraph wires were cut and tracks were torn up by Stuart's Cavalry.[17]

## 24 SHARPSBURG

Cole's First Maryland Cavalry skirmished with Southern horsemen during Lee's advance into Pennsylvania.[18]

## 28 EDWARDS FERRY

Stuart crossed the Potomac River at Edwards Ferry with three brigades of cavalry. His men burned several boats on the Chesapeake and Ohio Canal before continuing on to Rockville.

### ROCKVILLE

Stuart entered Rockville at 11 a.m. He soon learned of a huge Federal wagon train moving toward him on the road from Washington. He hoped to capture the entire train, but as soon as the drivers and escort troops caught sight of the Rebel cavalry, they wheeled about and galloped madly toward the safety of the Nation's capitol. Troopers of the Ninth Virginia charged after them, and soon were in among the wagons. Drivers abandoned their teams and ran into the woods to hide. Mules stampeded and wagons overturned in the uncontrolled effort to escape. Near the outskirts of Washington, the quartermaster in charge was captured. What was left of the regiment turned around and trotted back to Rockville, burning the disabled wagons along the way.[19]

Stuart's prize was 125 new wagons, over 700 mules and two ambulances. Most of the wagons contained corn and oats, but a few held cargoes of bread, bacon and whiskey, to the delight of the Rebels. Union losses numbered nearly 400, most of whom were captured.[20]

## FREDERICK CITY

General George Gordon Meade was given command of the Army of the Potomac. He relieved General Hooker just three days before the Battle of Gettysburg.

## 29 PINEY RUN BRIDGE

Stuart's cavalry burned the railroad bridge and destroyed the telegraph.[21]

## COOKSVILLE

Stuart's cavalry chased a small Union force out of town and captured several men who claimed to belong to "Seven Hundred Loyal Eastern Shoremen."[22] This detachment was actually from the First Eastern Shore Infantry Regiment.

## 29-30 WESTMINSTER

After capturing the wagon train at Rockville, Stuart moved north across central Maryland in search of Lee's Army. Approaching Westminster from the east, his advance guard captured five men from the First Delaware Cavalry at a blacksmith's shop. Alerted to the presence of enemy troops, he sent the Fourth Virginia Regiment to occupy the town.

Westminster was guarded by only two companies of Delaware Cavalry commanded by Major N.B. Knight and a small provost guard of the One Hundred and Fiftieth New York Infantry commanded by Lieutenant P. Bowman. Learning of the presence of Stuart, the Union cavalry mounted and began to advance toward the enemy on Main Street. Captain Charles Corbit of Company C ordered Lieutenant D.W.C. Clark to take 12 men and move ahead, in order to locate the enemy. Clark's detail ran smack into the Fourth Virginia and were soon driven back on the main force.

Corbit, showing more than a little courage, led Company C in a saber charge against an entire Rebel regiment. Soon Company D and the New Yorkers joined the small, violent battle that raged at the intersection of Main Street and Washington Road.[23]

In a few minutes, the three Union commanders and most of their men, were prisoners. Major Knight escaped with a fraction of his men. He later reported the loss of 67 men out of a command of only 95.[24] Two officers from the Fourth Virginia were killed in the battle. Stuart spent the night gathering forage and information. Early the next morning, he marched cross country toward Hanover, Pennsylvania.[25]


**30** RIDGEVILLE
The First Eastern Shore Infantry had just made camp on a hill overlooking the village of Ridgeville when firing broke out on the picket line. Confederates were crowding in on the Yankee's camp when the Ringgold Battery came up to support the Union line. Finally, Kilpatrick's troopers counter attacked and drove off the Rebel cavalry.[26]

# JULY 1863

Often written off with one or two sentences or entirely forgotten by many historians is the fact that the Gettysburg Campaign did not end with Pickett's charge. On the 4th of July, Lee held his ground and waited to see what the new commander of the Army of the Potomac would do, the same way he had waited out McClellan at Antietam. The difference at Antietam was the fact that Lee was only a few miles from the river, with fords passable and bridges intact. This time, the Confederates were a two to three day march from the Potomac. The presence of General William H. French's command at Frederick City, and the destruction of the bridge at Harpers Ferry, limited Lee's avenue of escape to the area west of those places. The first Southern units to reach the Potomac found the pontoon bridge cut up by Union cavalry, and the river well above fording at all near-by points. Between the 5th and the 14th of July, Lee fought a dozen battles in Western Maryland to fend off the pursuing Yankees. It is a fact, that for a week following the Battle of Gettysburg, the Army of Northern Virginia was in constant danger of being annihilated before it could recross the Potomac River.

## 5  EMMITSBURG

Jeb Stuart with the brigades of Chamblis and Jenkins, moved south from Gettysburg on July 3rd in the direction of Emmitsburg. His troops entered the town about dawn on the 5th.[27] They captured one officer, 66 enlisted men and some hospital supplies.[28]

In scouting the town before its capture, a detachment of the Seventh Virginia Cavalry was fired on by Union pickets and Private Peter Hulve of Company H was wounded.[29]

## SMITHSBURG

Having captured Ewell's wagon train in Pennsylvania, Kilpatrick moved his command south to Smithsburg. He arrived at 9 a.m. with 1,360 prisoners, one captured battle flag and a large number of horses and mules. After feeding the men, he placed them in defense positions on three hills that commanded the approaches to the town.[30]

Stuart's command approached from the direction of Emmitsburg late in the afternoon. He hoped to place himself between Lee's wagon train and the pursuing Union cavalry. Battery C, Third U.S. Artillery, fired three case shots to open the engagement. The Confederates answered with six guns from a distance of one mile. The long-range artillery duel lasted about one hour.[31] Unable to penetrate the Union defenses, Stuart broke off the engagement and retreated before nightfall. Neither side reported any losses.[32]

LEITERSBURG

Lieutenant Colonel A.W. Preston in command of the First Vermont Cavalry caught up with the rear most section of Lee's wagon train at Leitersburg. Preston captured 100 men, a drove of cattle and several wagons. The main part of the train had passed that point on its way to Hagerstown earlier.[33]


## 6 HAGERSTOWN

Colonel John R. Chamblis ordered the Ninth Virginia Regiment to enter Hagerstown in advance of his cavalry brigade. The Virginians found the town unoccupied, and were in the process of establishing picket posts when General Judson Kilpatrick's Third Cavalry Division was observed approaching along the Williamsport Road. A stubborn defense by the pickets gave Colonel J.L. Davis the opportunity to deploy his Tenth Virginia Regiment across the town's main street.[34]

Leading the Federal advance was the First Brigade, commanded by Colonel Nathaniel P. Richmond. Richmond ordered two squadrons of the Eighteenth Pennsylvania and one from the First West Virginia Cavalry to clear the town of Rebels. Charging in on the heels of the retreating pickets, they collided with the Tenth Virginia. In the insuing melee, Davis' horse was killed. With saber in hand, he fought on foot until captured.[35]

The force of the Union charge drove the Southerners back to the edge of town where infantry from Iverson's brigade opened fire from behind a stone wall and drove off their antagonists. Rallying behind the infantry, those men with carbines dismounted, and led by Captain Hayes, re-entered Hagerstown on foot to drive out the Yankees street by street.

During the fighting around the market place, a detachment of the First West Virginia Cavalry, charged up Main Street. Hayes' men greeted them with a volley that killed their leader. Continuing through town, they received a second volley from the infantry still posted behind the stone wall. Several horses and men were wounded and the balance of the attacking party captured.[36]

At the same time, the street fighting was going on, a Confederate battery began to shell the Union positions from a hill behind the town. Lieutenant Sam Elder's Battery E, supplied counter battery fire and blew up one casson. In return, Rebel sharpshooters killed and wounded several artillery horses, causing the Union battery to change position.

Stuart arrived with three brigades of cavalry and his horse artillery. Roberts' and Jenkins' brigades were ordered to push the enemy down the Williamsport Road as rapidly as possible. The attack hit a snag when Kilpatrick's men reformed along a rocky ridge and began to shell the road. Jenkins' men dismounted and charged over fences and across the difficult terrain to drive them out.[37]

As the Union withdrew toward Poolesville, the rear guard turned to fight about two miles outside of Hagerstown. One gun from Elder's battery was placed in the middle of the Williamsport Road. Its right flank was covered by the First Vermont and the left by the Fifth New York Cavalry.[38]

The Ninth Virginia charged head-long down the road in an attempt to capture the gun. The last round of cannister fired from the piece hit Sergeant Richard Washington, "...not twenty paces from the muzzel."[39] Another trooper was dismounted by one of the artillerymen who struck him with a sponge rod. Only the stubborn resistance by two squadrons of Union cavalry firing from behind a stone wall prevented the gun from being taken. Those troopers were finally driven off by a charge from the Eleventh Virginia Cavalry led by Colonel L.L. Lomax.[40]

Union losses were reported at 15 killed and 108 missing.[41] During the street fighting in Hagerstown, 16 men of the First Vermont were cut off from their command. Citizens loyal to the Federal Government concealed them for six days while awaiting the return of the Union Army.[42]

The importance of this battle was not the occupation of Hagerstown by either side, but in Stuart's prevention of Kilpatrick's division from joining forces with Buford in the latest attack on the Confederate wagon train at Williamsport.


WILLIAMSPORT

General John D. Imboden arrived on the 5th of July with a wagon train of wounded Confederates 17 miles long. He had left Gettysburg late on the 4th amidst a tremendous thunderstorm. The train had been on the move and in constant danger since its departure. Upon reaching Williamsport, Imboden learned the Potomac

River was 10 feet above fording.[43] The pontoon bridge left behind when Lee entered Maryland, had been set adrift by a raiding party from General French's command at Frederick City.[44]

Entrusted to Imboden were several thousand wounded soldiers, 10,000 draft animals and nearly all of the wagons of Lee's Army. His provisions consisted of a few wagons of flour, and some sugar and coffee taken at Mercersburg, and a small drove of cattle collected while in Pennsylvania. To protect this vast array of men and wagons he had, but, his own brigade of cavalry, 2,100 strong and 19 pieces of artillery.

Williamsport was quickly converted into one vast hospital camp. All the women in the area were ordered to cook for the wounded; some had not eaten in 36 hours. Surgeons accompanying the train began to relieve the suffering of the wounded. Those who had not survived the trip were buried.

Fortunately for the Confederates, an ordnance train from Winchester arrived on the opposite side of the river the same day. With it were two regiments of infantry and a number of miscellaneous troops returning to their commands. Imboden seized two flat boats and began ferrying his walking wounded to the Virginia shore. On the return trip, the boats brought back ammunition and badly needed infantry support.

The Confederate wagon train was still extremely vulnerable. Union cavalry was known to be in pursuit and could approach the town by at least three different roads. Imboden's command was not of sufficient strength to resist a major attack. Furthermore, Lee and Stuart were not yet within supporting distance. To augment his forces, Imboden ordered the wagon drivers armed with weapons taken from the wounded. By noon, seven 100-men companies were formed, commanded by commissary, quartermaster and wounded line officers.[45]

One of the premier artillery units of the Civil War was the Washington Artillery of New Orleans. Eight guns of this battalion under the command of Major B.F. Eshleman, were placed in the center of the Confederate line to cover both the Boonsboro and Hagerstown Roads. Between these two roads, two rifled guns from Barnett's battalion and a section of 12-pound Howitzers from Hart's battery were positioned. The last four guns mentioned were dangerously short of ammunition. The Donaldsonville Battery was posted on Greencastle Road with Imboden's guns filling in on both flanks toward the river.[46]

To support the artillery, Imboden dismounted his entire brigade and placed it in the center of his line. A makeshift battalion of drivers and wounded was sent to the right under Colonel William A. Aylett. Colonel John L. Black took a similar number of men to the left, while the remainder of Imboden's infantry were sent out as skirmishers.[47]

At 4 a.m. on the 6th, Buford's First Cavalry Division left Frederick to attack the Confederate wagon train at Williamsport. Buford was supported by Merritt's brigade and a number of batteries. The Union advance drove in the Rebel picket at St. James College and caught a small convoy outside the Rebel line. Seven wagonloads of grain were burned and about 50 mules captured.[48]

Late in the afternoon, dismounted cavalry advanced along both the Hagerstown and Boonsboro Roads. Three-quarters of the First Brigade advanced to the left of the Boonsboro Road, supported by four guns of Tidball's battery.[49]

Moore and Hart's batteries quickly used up their scant supply of ammunition and were withdrawn. Lacking long-range artillery, Eshleman advanced Miller's battery 600 yards with only a skirmish line for support. Yankee sharpshooters began popping away at the artillerymen from a house on Miller's right flank. The fire of a Napolean under Captain Narcom was directed at the structure after which a charge by a Southern infantry secured it for the remainder of the battle.

Fighting was also severe on the Confederate left flank. A single gun crew in Lieutenant Samuel Hane's section had 12 men killed or wounded.[50] Two guns of Courtney's Virginia Artillery fought until their ammunition was exhausted and most of their horses were killed.[51] Imboden shifted his dismounted cavalry from behind the Washington Artillery and counter attacked on the right. He captured 125 dismounted Yankees before they could reach their horses. At the same time, Black's wagoneers advanced on the left as the Confederate artillery blazed away all along the line. The Union advance was checked. Receiving reports that several of his units were running out of ammunition, Buford broke off the action and withdrew near nightfall. His decision to retreat was reinforced by the belief that the Confederate force in his front was much larger than in reality. Shortly after dark, Fitzhugh Lee's cavalry brigade arrived and the crisis was temporarily over.[52]

Union losses were reported at 14 killed, 50 wounded and 195 missing.[53] Imboden estimated his total casualties at 125.[54]

# 7 DOWNSVILLE

As more Confederate troops arrived in the Williamsport area, Stuart began to set up an outer line of defense to screen the wagon train from future Union assaults. At Downsville, he posted General William T. Wofford's infantry brigade on loan from Longstreet's corps.[55]

Union cavalry skirmished with those units on July 7 and lost one man killed and one man wounded.[56]

## FUNKSTOWN

The Sixth United States Cavalry, commanded by Captain Ira W. Claflin, was on a reconnaissance patrol when it encountered a Confederate outpost. Leading the advance guard, Claflin drove the Rebels back to the edge of the town. During the attack, he was wounded in the shoulder and the command devolved on Lieutenant Nicholas Nolon.[57]

The Union cavalry had encountered the Seventh Virginia Cavalry, a regiment it had bested in the fighting at Fairfield, Pennsylvania a few days earlier. Lieutenant Colonel Thomas Marshall ordered his Virginians to counter attack and a sharp, running fight ensued.[58] Sergeant John McCaffery of Company A shot a Southern standard bearer, but was driven off before he could capture the flag.[59] Sergeant Thomas Dodd of Company B, received a saber wound to the head, but managed to escape capture.[60] The Confederates, anxious to avenge their defeat at Fairfield, pursued the Federals for almost five miles. They captured about 50 prisoners and a great number of horses and weapons.

Fearing his men's enthusiasm would carry them beyond a safe distance, Marshall ordered a halt, which was not at first heeded. Reaching the front of his column, Marshall sent those men with jaded horses to a good defensive position in the rear. He held his ground with a few better mounted men and sent a courier to General Jones.

The Yankees sensed the condition of their pursuers. Turning

about, they attacked Marshall's small party, which fired a single volley and ran for the protection of the main force. The men in the rear in turn, opened fire and emptied a number of saddles, but were unable to resist the Union charge. The Confederates had only two men wounded and nine captured. Nolon reported 59 killed, wounded or captured, and stated that 10 bodies were recovered later in the day by the First United States Cavalry.[61]

## MARYLAND HEIGHTS

After the battle of Winchester, Virginia on June 15, what was left of Milroy's command retreated to Maryland Heights where they were joined with the garrison at Harpers Ferry in improving their defense positions. The combined forces were commanded by Major General William H. French.

On June 29, French received orders to evacuate Harpers Ferry and Maryland Heights. Government property was sent to Washington via the Chesapeake and Ohio Canal, guarded by several thousand men. French fell back to Frederick City with the balance of his command to keep communications open between Washington and the Army of the Potomac. The Confederates were not given a second chance to bag the garrison at Harpers Ferry as they had done during the Antietam Campaign.

Shortly after the Federal withdrawal, Confederate troops occupied Maryland Heights. They immediately began to gather stores and equipment left behind by the retreating Yankees. They also set about repairing the railroad bridge which had been partially destroyed by Cole's cavalry.

On July 6, French sent the Maryland Brigade commanded by General John R. Kenly to re-occupy Maryland Heights. Kenly's command consisted of the First, Fourth, and Eighth Maryland Volunteers and Miner's Seventeenth Indiana Battery. The assault force spent the night in Knoxville, a small town at the southern end of Pleasant Valley. The next day, Kenly sent the First Maryland Volunteers up the east slope of Maryland Heights. He led the balance of his command up river along the Chesapeake and Ohio Canal. Two companies of the Fourth Maryland formed the advance guard. As these men neared the base of Maryland Heights, they found the road barricaded and the Confederates opened fire. The balance of the two regiments were immediately advanced to their support.

At the same time, one section of Miner's guns began to shell Confederate cavalry on Bolivar Heights. The Union attack was aided by the arrival of an armored train from Baltimore containing seven light field pieces and infantry. The railroad battery began to shell Rebel sharpshooters on the Virginia side of the Potomac River. The heights were soon taken and a picket line established from the river to Solomon's Gap.[62]

## 8 BOONSBORO

In order to cover the concentration of Lee's Army at Williamsport, Jeb Stuart advanced five brigades of cavalry along a wide front toward Boonsboro. Jones' brigade encountered Union cavalry at Beaver Creek Bridge. Because heavy rains had left the surrounding field only a little better than marshland, Jones was forced to dismount his men and attack as infantry. Jenkins' brigade struck the Union flank along the Williamsport Road.[63]

At 11:30 in the morning, General Kilpatrick reported to the Union cavalry commander that Merritt's brigade had been pushed back to the edge of Boonsboro, and Buford's command was preparing to withdraw to the mountain range behind the town.[64] Learning of the attack, Meade ordered Major General O.O. Howard to move his Eleventh Corps to the top of South Mountain. The Sixth Corps was held in reserve. Union artillery prevented the Southern cavalry from ever entering Boonsboro. With his troops running low on ammunition, and Yankee infantry crowding the top of South Mountain, Stuart broke off the engagement and retreated with the bulk of his command to Funkstown. Jenkins' brigade returned to its former position on the Williamsport Road.[65]

Major General Carl Schurz's infantry division with one battery, and Buford's cavalry followed up the Confederate withdraw.[66] As the First North Carolina Cavalry was crossing over the bridge at Beaver Creek, it was attacked by a squadron of Union cavalry. Before the two units could come into contact with each other, the Union troopers were driven off by the accurate fire of a Blakely gun from Chew's battery.[67]

WILLIAMSPORT ROAD

Brigadier General B.F. Kelly ordered Captain Andrew J.

Greenfield to take his company of cavalry and scout the area around McCoy's Ferry and Clear Springs. Coming upon a Confederate supply train, Greenfield pursued and captured it four miles from Williamsport.

He took two officers and 20 enlisted men prisoner, and captured 80 mules, but was forced to leave the wagons behind.[68] Union losses were reported as four enlisted men wounded and three horses killed.[69]

## BEAVER CREEK [BENEVULA]

The day after Stuart's attack on Boonsboro, Union cavalry advanced from that town, a distance of two to three miles, in anticipation of a renewed attack. After waiting most of the day, the First Cavalry Division was ordered to cross Beaver Creek and establish contact with the enemy. The time was 5:30 p.m. Supported by artillery, Union cavalry succeeded in driving the enemy from their camp and defensive position along the crest of a hill. Colonel Thomas C. Devin led the Second Brigade in pursuit of the Rebels for a distance of two miles when nightfall put an end to the action.[70]

**10** CLEAR SPRINGS

On July 7, the Seventy-Fourth Regiment New York National Guard commanded by Colonel Watson A. Fox, and three companies of the Twenty-Ninth Pennsylvania Infantry, under Colonel Joseph W. Hawley, were ordered to move from Loudon, Pennsylvania to Clear Springs, Maryland. Attached to this command was one company of the Twelfth Pennsylvania Cavalry commanded by Captain Nathaniel Payne.

At 8 a.m. on the 10th, Payne's company left its camp in Bear Valley to make a reconnaissance toward Clear Springs. When it neared the town, it became engaged with a force of Confederate cavalry. The action lasted until the arrival of the two infantry units, at which time the Rebels retreated. Payne had three men wounded, one of which died the next day. Fox reported four of his enemy wounded.[71]

## LEITERSBURG

The First Brigade, Second Cavalry Division, under the command of Colonel John B. McIntosh, was ordered to scout the area along Antietam Creek and Leitersburg. Three miles west of Leitersburg, the Union cavalry struck a Confederate picket post and drove·it across Antietam Creek to a position well defended by the Rebel Infantry and Artillery.[72]

## 10-20 FUNKSTOWN

Having recovered from the surprise engagement at Boonsboro two days earlier, the Union cavalry set out again on the 10th to harass the retreating Army of Northern Virginia. Buford dismounted his division and advanced along the National Pike with Merritt's brigade on the right, Devin's on the left and Gamble's in the center. Two sections of Tidball's light artillery provided fire support. To check the Union advance, Stuart had most of his cavalry plus Campbell's battalion of artillery, and two brigades of infantry from Longstreet's corps. The infantry were placed on either side of the turnpike running from Funkstown to Beaver Creek. Stuart's right flank extended toward Antietam Creek, just north of a large stone barn on the Hauck farm. His left rested on the Smithburg Road near the old Kemp house. Dismounted cavalry and Chew's horse artillery protected both flanks.

The Union attack began at 8 a.m. and soon drove the Southern skirmish line back to the edge of town. Here it encountered a steady fire from sharpshooters in Stonebreaker's barn and from dismounted cavalry behind a stone wall on the Hauck farm.

A portion of Buford's command occupied Stover's Woods, where they were joined by part of the Vermont Brigade and guns from the Third New York and First Rhode Island Artillery. Union sharpshooters advanced as far as Stover's barn. To counter this threat, Colonel White, acting commander of Anderson's brigade, led a counter attack which cleared the barn and two fields of Yankees, but failed to dislodge the main force in the woods.[73]

By 3:00 in the afternoon, several of the Union units began to run out of ammunition and were forced to withdraw from the high ground near the town which they had seized in the morning. These positions were re-occupied by the Confederates before nightfall.[74] The intensity of the battle is reflected in the number of killed, wounded and missing assigned to the following units.[75]

| UNION | Vermont Brigade | 97 |
|---|---|---|
| | Buford's Cavalry | 99 |
| CONFEDERATE | Anderson's Brigade | 127 |
| | Stuart's Cavalry | 156 |
| | TOTAL | 479 |

During the night, the Union infantry camped only a short distance from the town. The next day saw only light skirmishing with neither side eager to advance.[76] On the 12th, Brigadier General Horatio G. Wright advanced with his First Division and Eustis' brigade at dawn and took possession of the town. The Union infantry then crossed Antietam Creek and attacked the Confederate positions on the high ground behind the town. During this part of the action, Captain R.W. Furlong led Company D of the Sixth Maine Infantry through the Southern skirmish line and captured an entire company of Confederates, numbering 35 men. Wright reported only eight men wounded in the engagement.[77]

## 11  JONES' CROSS-ROADS

On the 11th, the First Brigade of Hay's division was sent on a reconnaissance toward Funkstown. This force clashed with Confederate pickets three miles from Jones' Cross-Roads. One man was slightly wounded.[78]

## 11-13  HAGERSTOWN

After skirmishing in the area for two days, the Union cavalry advanced along the several roads leading to Hagerstown. Early on the morning of the 13th, Stuart's cavalry offered very little resistance as it retreated through the town to the safety of entrenched infantry on the National Road.[79] During this retreat, Union cavalry struck the rear of the Twelfth Virginia from the two side streets in town. One Confederate was killed and three wounded.[80]

When Lee's Army reached Hagerstown, the pioneers of each division were sent to Williamsport to begin reconstructing the pontoon bridge. Materials from a nearby lumber yard were confiscated and in two days, 16 pontoon boats were built. The boats were loaded with lumber and floated down river to Falling Waters, where they were joined together with 10 of the original pontoon boats not destroyed by the Yankee raiding party. As soon as the bridge was completed, Lee's army began crossing the river in earnest.[81]

# 14 WILLIAMSPORT

The Fifth Michigan Cavalry charged into town on the morning of the 14th and captured a number of stragglers.[82]

## FALLING WATERS

Lee intended to cross most, if not all, of his army over the Potomac on the night of the 13th. Due to adverse conditions of both weather and terrain, this was not accomplished until 1 p.m. on the 14th. The prolonged withdrawal gave the Union army an opportunity to engage the Southerner's rear guard, greatly increasing their losses for the campaign.[83]

One of the units left to cover Lee's retreat was Archer's Tennessee Brigade, commanded at the time by Colonel S.G. Shepard. During the night of the 13th, Archer's brigade pulled out of its position between Hagerstown and Williamsport. Moving the artillery proved to be a difficult task and slowed the infantry's pace, so that, by daybreak they were still five miles from the Potomac. Shepard urged his men on until they reached the crest of the hill two miles from the river. Here he halted to rest his men and cover the crossing of the guns.[84]

Union infantry and cavalry advanced on the morning of July 14 to find the enemy's works abandoned. Kilpatrick's Third Cavalry Division caught up with Archer's brigade about 7:30 a.m. His advanced units captured one gun and its infantry supports about 1000 yards in front of the main body. Believing the Rebels easy prey, Major Weber led Companies A and B of the Sixth Michigan Cavalry in a saber charge against the First Tennessee Infantry.[85]

The First Tennessee was resting behind some earthworks and did not realize that Weber's men were Yankees until the latter was quite close to their position. Most of their weapons were stacked and unloaded, as were the rest of the brigade's; a most unusual ploy for a rear guard unit. When the cavalry reached the breastworks, the infantry beat them off with clubbed muskets and a few scattered shots. Veering off, the Union cavalry caught a volley from the rest of Archer's brigade, which by now, had most of its guns loaded.[86] Companies A and B lost 30 men, including Major Peter A. Weber and Lieutenant Charles E. Bolza, who were killed in the charge.[87] The Confederate infantry lost only one killed and seven wounded.[88] Of greater significance was the death of the rear guard commander, Brigadier General James J. Pettigrew. Pettigrew was the 10th and last general officer killed on Maryland soil during the Civil War.

As Union forces continued to press Lee's rear guard, General Harry Heath counter marched Scale's brigade to their support. In the course of the changing positions, the troops that were to be helped were withdrawn and Scale's brigade was cut off. Colonel W.L.J. Lawrence, commanding the brigade, immediately ordered his men to file to the rear and reached the river three-fourths of a mile above the bridge. While moving down the river, the Yankees penetrated a wooden area and cut off nearly 200 Southerners before they could reach the bridge.[89]

The final rear guard action of the Gettysburg Campaign was fought by Lane's brigade. Heath ordered Lane to cover the retreat of his beaten division, and then fall back to the river. Lieutenant Colonel James Crowell's Twenty-Eighth North Carolina was the last element of Lee's army to cross the Potomac River.[90] As they did so, cables that anchored the bridge to the Maryland shore were cut. The force of the current pushed the floating structure like the hand of a giant clock over to the Virginia side of the river.

That night, Confederate pioneers crept down the river bank and pulled out the 10 good boats. These were loaded on wagons and sent to the rear. The pontoons built at Williamsport were scuttled to prevent them from being used by the enemy.[91] Thus ended the Gettsyburg Campaign.

## 20  POINT LOOKOUT PRISON ESTABLISHED

Following the Battle of Gettysburg, the Federal Government established a prisoner of war camp at Point Lookout for the thousands of Confederates taken prisoner in July of 1863.[92] By April of 1865, 20,110 Rebel prisoners crowded the desert-like peninsula where the Potomac River meets the Chesapeake Bay.[93] An estimated

4,000 men died there during their internment, a record that rivals the more famous Confederate prison at Andersonville, Georgia.[94]

# AUGUST 1863

**17** THE GREAT WICOMICO RIVER
The *U.S.S. Satellite,* under the command of Acting Master John F.D. Robinson, seized the schooner *Three Brothers* on the Great Wicomico River.[95]

**27** EDWARDS FERRY
Colonel E.V. White and 150 men of the Thirty-Fifth Virginia Battalion, crossed the Potomac River above Edwards Ferry on the night of August 27. Their objective was to attack a fortified camp at the ferry, manned by a unit called "Scott's 900." The Confederates attempted to surprise the camp from the rear, but failed when a picket fired a shot and was in turn killed. Most of the Union troops escaped, but 12 men and all the camp equipment was captured.[96]

# SEPTEMBER 1863

**3** Publication of the *Baltimore Republican* was suppressed. The editor and owner were sent across the lines by order of Major General Robert Schenck. Schenck commanded the Middle Department from August 30, 1862 to December 5, 1863.[97]

## 15 PRESIDENT LINCOLN SUSPENDS THE WRIT OF *HABEAS CORPUS*

Acting on the powers granted by Congress, Lincoln issued the following proclamation:

> "Now, therefore, I, Abraham Lincoln, President of the United States, do hereby proclaim and make known to all whom it may concern, that the privileges of the Writ of *Habeas Corpus* is suspended throughout the United States..."[98]

The illegal political arrests in Maryland were now officially legal.

## 16 POTOMAC RIVER

The *U.S.S. Coeur DeLion,* under the command of Acting Master W.G. Morris, captured the schooner *Robert Knowles* while the latter vessel was attempting to run the blockade on the Potomac River.

## 19-23 BEALL'S EXPEDITION TO THE CHESAPEAKE BAY

Acting Master John F. Beall, Confederate States Navy, in company with Acting Master Edward McGuire, led a small boat expedition into the Chesapeake Bay. On September 19, they captured the schooner *Alliance* with a cargo of sutler's stores. Two days later, the Rebels seized another schooner, the *J.J. Houseman.* On the night of September 22, the Confederates captured two more schooners, the *Samuel Pearsall* and the *Alexandria.* Beall stopped at Wachapreague Inlet long enough to cast three of his four prizes adrift. He then attempted to run the blockade back into Virginia aboard the *Alliance* with its cargo of sutler's items.

On the morning of September 23, the *Alliance* ran aground at Milford Haven. Before she could be freed, the *U.S.S. Thomas Freeborn* discovered the stranded vessel and opened fire. Beall set fire to the ship to prevent its recapture and made good his escape.[99]

**23** ROCKVILLE
One of the ironies of the Civil War was visited on the community of Rockville in September of 1863. A column of Confederate cavalry crossed the Potomac River about four miles from the town. The Rebels stopped to feed their horses in a corn field near the farm of Alexander Kilgore. Having refreshed their mounts, the Confederates advanced about a mile and a half when they collided with a patrol from "Scott's 900" with infantry supports. In the fighting that ensued, 34 Rebels were killed or wounded, including the commanding officer, Captain Frank Kilgore. Outnumbered, the Confederates broke off the engagement and returned to Virginia.[100]

# OCTOBER 1863

**9** Lincoln issued a proclamation making the last Thursday in November a national day of Thanksgiving. Governor Bradford subsequently issued a statewide proclamation as did several other leaders of Northern states. This led to the holiday as we know it today.

**17** Lincoln called for 300,000 volunteers to serve for three years. State quotas not filled by volunteers on or before January 5, 1864 were to be filled by the draft.

**21** BENEDICT
Lieutenant Eben White sailed from Baltimore on October 19 with two companies of the Seventh United States Colored Troops. The following day he landed at Benedict in Charles County and established a recruiting station. On the 21st he learned that Colonel John H. Southron had two of his slaves tied up at his home a mile below the town to prevent their enlisting in the Union Army. That afternoon he took two men and proceeded to the Southron estate where he was confronted by the colonel and his son — both armed with shotguns and pistols. When Lt. White attempted to enlist a gang of slaves working in a nearby field, Southron engaged White in a

heated debate that ended in gun play. White was shot twice in the chest and died. One of his men and the colonel's son were both slightly wounded.

The soldiers returned to camp and reported to Captain Leary of the *Cecil* what had transpired. Leary returned to the plantation with a detachment of soldiers and sailors. He found White's body with two additional bullet wounds and his head bashed in. Colonel Southron and his family were gone. It was later learned they had fled to Richmond.

# NOVEMBER 1863

**4** MARYLAND STATE ELECTION DAY
Ever fearful of Southern interference or a Democratic victory, Major General Schenck, the commander of the Middle Department, issued General Order 53, which directed all provost marshals and unit commanders to arrest any persons suspected or known to be disloyal to the Union. This order was ridiculed by Governor Bradford and defended by President Lincoln.[101]

**22** ST. GEORGE'S ISLAND
On November 22, the *U.S.S. Jacob Bell* was involved in an amphibious operation at St. George's Island. As Union infantry boarded small boats and made for the island, Acting Master Gerhard C. Schulze covered their progress with the guns of the *Jacob Bell*. When the troops landed, they quickly rounded up 30 Confederate soldiers and blockade runners who had been using the island as a base of operations.[102]

**29** PATUXENT RIVER
In the latter part of November Lieutenants Thompson, Mack, Cheney, and Califf of the Seventh United States Colored Troops, along with Sergeants Yeaton and Swift, boarded the steam tugs *Balloon* and *Cecil* at Benedict. The next day they began to raid the Oyster Fleet then laying at the mouth of the Patuxent River and in Tangier Sound. Ten days later this little flotilla returned with 130 recruits for their regiment.

# CHAPTER SIX
# 1864

During the summer of 1864, the Confederacy mounted its third and final invasion of Maryland by way of the Shenandoah Valley. Frederick City was ransomed, and Washington was placed under siege, while Rebel cavalry roamed north and south of Baltimore, bringing the war to parts of the state left untouched during the previous three years. In mid-July, Lieutenant General Jubal A. Early's troops recrossed the Potomac River as Union forces converged on them from three directions. By the end of the year, Early's army would be destroyed, and the Shenandoah Valley laid waste due to the aggressive actions of Major General Phillip H. Sheridan. From July of 1864 until the surrender of Lee's army at Appomattox in the spring of 1865, military operations in the state of Maryland became less frequent and were usually the work of Mosby, Gilmor, McNeill or White's independent commands.

# JANUARY 1864

**6** ANNAPOLIS
The State Legislature convened on January 6, 1864. Its first order of business was to fill a vacancy in the U.S. Senate caused by the death of James Alfred Pierce, in the previous December. Former Governor Thomas Holliday Hicks was elected to serve out Pierce's term.

A more momentous undertaking was the introduction of a bill calling for a state convention for the purpose of abolishing slavery. It will be remembered that Lincoln's Emancipation Proclamation only applied to those states that had left the Union. Therefore, slavery still existed in Maryland in 1864.[1]

# FEBRUARY 1864

**4** CHESAPEAKE BAY
The *U.S. Revenue Steamer Hercules* seized the schooner *Ann Hamilton* off Point Lookout. Salt, lye and over $15,000 in Confederate currency was found on board. Commander Foxhall A. Parker of the Potomac Flotilla ordered the vessel to Washington for adjudication.[2]

# MARCH 1864

**10** Lieutenant General Ulysses S. Grant was given command of all armies of the United States.[3]

**12** Major General Lew Wallace was appointed commander of the Eighth Army Corps and the Middle Department, with headquarters in Baltimore.[4]

# APRIL 1864

**6** Marylanders voted to determine if a Constitutional Convention would be held to address the slavery issue. The vote was 31,593 for and 19,524 against.

**27** ANNAPOLIS
The long debated Constitutional Convention convened in Annapolis on April 27, 1864. Henry H. Goldsborough, of Talbot County, was elected president of the convention. Goldsborough was also the state comptroller at the time. The convention lasted for four months and did not adjourn until September 6, 1864.[5]

# MAY 1864

**11-14** EXPEDITION FROM POINT LOOKOUT TO THE RAPPAHANNOCK RIVER, VIRGINIA
The object of the raid was to search for enemy troops and supplies along with the removal of torpedoes [mines] from the water.[6]

**19** BLACKISTONE ISLAND
On the night of May 19, a small boat landed on Blackistone Island at Piney Point. John M. Goldsmith led a raiding party of 12 men against the lighthouse there. They ransacked the lighthouse, destroyed the lamp and lens, and carried off 15 gallons of oil.[7]

**22** SEVERN RIVER
The *U.S.S. Crusader*, under the command of Lieutenant Peter Hays, captured the schooner *Isaac L. Adkins* at the mouth of the Severn River. The schooner was carrying a cargo of corn and oats.[8]

**24** FORT MCHENRY
Andrew Leopole of Washington County, Maryland, was hung at Fort McHenry. Leopole was noted for his spying and guerilla activities throughout the upper Potomac River area.[9]

# JUNE 1864

**4** POTOMAC RIVER
The *U.S.S. Ceour DeLion*, under the command of Acting Master William G. Morris, seized the schooner *Malinda* for violating the blockade on the Potomac River.[10]

**7** BALTIMORE
The National Union Party held its presidential convention in Baltimore at the Front Street Theater. Abraham Lincoln was unanimously nominated on the first ballot. Andrew Johnson of Tennessee was nominated for vice-president.[11]

**9** POINT OF ROCKS
The Second United States Colored Cavalry had two men killed in an engagement with the enemy.[12]

# JULY 1864

**4** POINT OF ROCKS
The mail train of the Baltimore and Ohio Railroad was attacked and the fireman was wounded. The engineer reversed his engine and returned safely to Sandy Hook.[13]

# 5-7 MARYLAND HEIGHTS

On the 4th of July, Confederate troops skirmished with Union pickets on Bolivar Heights, West Virginia.

Brigadier General Max Weber, the post commander at Harpers Ferry, ordered all government property sent across the river to Sandy Hook. At 7 p.m., a Federal signal station reported a large force of Rebel troops approaching from Halltown. Weber ordered Harpers Ferry evacuated and moved his garrison to Maryland Heights. He was joined that night by General Franz Sigel's command from Martinsburg. After skirmishing with the Union troops for three days, the Confederates withdrew on the 7th. Harpers Ferry was re-occupied by Federal troops on the 8th of July.[14]

# 5 KEEDYSVILLE

Listed in the Summary of Principal Events, "Official Records," Series I, Volume 37, p. 169.

## NOLAND'S FERRY

The Eighth Illinois Cavalry prevented the Confederate cavalry, led by Mosby, from crossing the Potomac River on the night of July 6, 1864.[15]

## SOLOMON'S GAP

Men of the Twenty-First New York Cavalry skirmished with the vanguard of Early's army.[16]

## POINT OF ROCKS

Learning of Early's advance down the Shenandoah Valley, Lieutenant Colonel John S. Mosby moved 250 men of his Forty-Third Virginia Battalion and one 12-pound Napoleon cannon east of the Blue Ridge Mountains, to be in a position to cooperate with the main Confederate Army as it entered Maryland. Crossing the Potomac River at Point of Rocks, Mosby drove out the Union garrison, consisting of two companies of Loudon Rangers and two companies of infantry. He captured several men, horses, and a large quantity of camp equipment.

As the Rebel cavalry splashed across the river, the Union troops retreated across the Chesapeake and Ohio Canal. After crossing the bridge, they pulled up the planks and took cover in a small earthwork behind the canal. Leading the Confederate charge, Captain A.E. Richards dismounted and replaced enough boards to allow his men to cross the bridge. Remounting, he renewed the attack and drove off the Union troops. During their stay in Point of Rocks, Mosby's men destroyed telegraph wires and poles and fired on a train, but failed to capture it.[17]

Colonel Clendenin's Eighth Illinois Cavalry arrived from Washington about 2 p.m. Clendenin dismounted half of his men and skirmished with the Rebels for about 30 minutes. Mosby fired half a dozen rounds from his 12-pounder and then returned with his command to Virginia.[18]


## 5-6 HAGERSTOWN

In 1861, Hagerstown was a good sized supply base for the Union Army. A large amount of stores, plus 500 to 700 horses were kept there. Lieutenant Draper commanded a garrison of 20 officers and 75 enlisted men. He learned that the Rebels had burned a number of boats at Slack Water on the 4th and consequently, he put his troops on alert.[19]

The quartermaster moved almost all of the government property and horses to Carlisle, Pennsylvania. All movable railroad equipment was sent north to Harrisburg.[20]

General John McCausland's cavalry advanced on the 5th along the Sharpsburg Turnpike and struck a Federal picket post three miles from town. The pickets quickly retreated and reported to Lieutenant Hancock T. McLean of the Sixth U.S. Cavalry. McLean sent a corporal and four men out with orders to engage the enemy and slowly fall back. When the Confederates reached the edge of town, McLean led a counter attack and captured one lieutenant and two privates. Several of his men were wounded in the charge.[21] Following this action, the Union garrison evacuated the town about 1 p.m.

General McCausland entered the town the next day and issued a written demand for $20,000 in U.S. money. He also demanded complete outfits of clothes and an additional 1900 pairs of pants. Three hours were given to collect the money, and four hours for the clothing. When the ransom was paid, McCausland realized that he had left out a digit — he had wanted $200,000. Taking the money and what clothing that had been collected, he led his command toward Frederick.

Shortly after McCausland left, a second group of Confederates rode into town, led by Major T. Sturgis Davis. They set fire to the government hay and the Franklin Railroad depot. They also demanded a second ransom of $500 to keep from burning private warehouses containing government property, but finally settled for a payment of 10 pairs of boots.[22]

## 6 ANTIETAM CREEK
Three companies of the Twelfth Pennsylvania skirmished with the Rebel forces and reported four men missing.[23]

### MIDDLETOWN
A scouting party composed of 75 men from the Twelfth Pennsylvania Cavalry and Mean's Loudon Rangers, commanded by Major Thorpe, and an additional 10 men from Cole's Cavalry, under Adjutant O.A. Horner, struck a Rebel picket post about one mile outside of Middletown. Horner and his small command led the charge and drove the enemy picket back on its reserve, about 25 strong. When the Confederates counter attacked, Thorpe turned tail and ran for the safety of Frederick City. Horner, realizing he was outnumbered, quickly broke off the action. During the retreat, his horse was killed, falling upon its rider and causing his capture.

Horner escaped later in the day and took refuge in an abandoned negroe's cabin. Shortly thereafter, the Confederate picket post was re-established in front of the very cabin he was hiding in. Undaunted, the adjutant donned a civilian hat and coat, and escaped out the back door. Horner walked back to Frederick City and rejoined his command.[24]

### BROWNSVILLE
Company E, Twenty-First New York Cavalry lost one man killed in skirmishes with Confederate forces.[25]

### MIDDLETOWN
At 5:30 in the morning, Colonel D.R. Clendenin rode out of

Frederick City at the head of the Eighth Illinois Cavalry. His regiment was supported by two guns from Alexander's Baltimore Light Artillery, under the command of Lieutenant Peter Leary. Clendenin had been ordered by Major General Lew Wallace to locate the invading Rebel Army.[26]

The Union reconnaissance encountered a brigade of Confederate cavalry two miles outside of Middletown. These troops were commanded by newly promoted Brigadier General Bradley T. Johnson. Johnson was a native Marylander and resident of Frederick before the war. As soon as the firing broke out, he brought up his reserves and began to push the Union cavalry back towards his home town.[27]

## HAGER'S MOUNTAIN [CATOCTIN MOUNTAIN]

Unable to penetrate the screen of Southern cavalry at Middletown, Clendenin withdrew his troops to Hager's Mountain. Here, Leary's guns were planted on the side of the mountain and opened fire as the Union cavalry skirmished for five hours with the lead elements of Early's army.[28]

## SOLOMON'S GAP [FREDERICK]

Bradley Johnson continued to push his men against the Union position at Hager's Mountain until Clendenin was forced to retreat a second time, which brought him to the suburbs of Frederick City. Clendenin notified Wallace that unless reinforced, Frederick would be in enemy hands by nightfall. As commander of the Middle Department, Wallace's authority stopped at the Monocacy River. To his credit, he did not succumb to bureaucracy, and he ordered a portion of his small army to protect the city.

When Clendenin reached Solomon's Gap, he met Captain F.W. Alexander with a fresh supply of ammunitions and a third gun from his battery. Clendenin cleared the road of his troopers, and ordered Alexander to shell the Rebel advance. At this time, Colonel Charles Gilpin arrived with the Third Regiment of the Potomac Home Brigade and 100 men of the One Hundred and Fifty-Ninth Ohio National Guard, a one hundred day regiment serving as mounted infantry. Gilpin ordered the cavalry to form on his left and fight dismounted. He placed his infantry in position across the Hagerstown Pike and waited for the enemy to make the next move.

At 4 p.m., the Confederates opened fire with three guns, which were soon followed by a general engagement. At 6 p.m., one of the Confederate field pieces was dismounted by a Parrott gun under the personal supervision of Alexander. Just before nightfall, Gilpin ordered his troops to advance and the Southern forces withdrew to the next mountain.[29] Union losses were reported as five killed and 20 wounded.[30]

Lew Wallace was evidently pleased with the outcome of the days fighting for that night he wrote, "Think I have had the best little battle of the war."[31] Little did he know that the next day he would fight the battle that would save the nation's capitol.

## 7-9 BALTIMORE
The Third Division of the Sixth Army Corps arrived at Locust Point. It then moved on trains provided by the Baltimore and Ohio Railroad to Monocacy Junction.

## 8 ANTIETAM BRIDGE
Captain Edwin Frey, with 40 men from the Second Cavalry Division, all of the cavalry then at Harpers Ferry, encountered a Confederate rear guard unit at Antietam Bridge. Captain Frey reported the main enemy force advancing on the Boonsboro Road past "John Brown's schoolhouse."[32]

## SKIRMISH AT SANDY HOOK
Listed in the Summary of Principal Events, "Official Records," Series I, Volume 27, Part I, p. 170.

## 8-9 FREDERICK
At midnight on the 7th, Wallace sent Brigadier General Erastus B. Tyler to take command of all Union forces in Frederick City. He was accompanied by four companies of the Ohio National Guard, commanded by Colonel A.L. Brown, while Wallace remained at Monocacy Junction. Near dawn on the 8th, the first elements of the Sixth Corps arrived from Baltimore; they were sent immediately to reinforce Tyler.[33]

Tyler spread his men across the Hagerstown Pike, near the same point they held the day before. Bradley Johnson's Confederates probed and pushed at the Federal line, but made no definite attack. Johnson hoped to hold the Yankees west of Monocacy River until Early's infantry could arrive and attack them with overwhelming numbers.[34]

At 6 p.m., Wallace received a report from Colonel Lynde Catlin, informing him that a heavy force of enemy infantry was approaching Urbana by the Buckeystown Road. This force threatened to cut off General Tyler's command and indicated that Early might be planning an assault on Washington. With Baltimore or the capitol at stake, Frederick became a secondary consideration. Wallace ordered the city evacuated that night.[35] Clendenin's cavalry covered the withdraw and did not leave until 2 a.m. on the 9th. In the two days of fighting near Frederick, the Eighth Illinois Cavalry lost four killed and 15 wounded.[36]

Confederate troops quickly occupied Frederick City after the Yankees pulled out. Shortly after 8 a.m., Mayor William G. Cole received the following communication from Early.

Fredericktown, Md., July 9, 1864

By order of the Lieut-Gen. Comdg:

We require of the mayor and town authorities $200,000 in current money for the use of the army.

If the money was not raised immediately, Early threatened to burn the city in retaliation for the destruction caused by General David Hunter in the Shenandoah Valley. For a community of only 8,000 inhabitants, this was no meager sum. Working with five different banks, the mayor was able to pay the ransom and the city was not burned.[37]

## 9 MONOCACY

To appreciate the outcome of the Battle of Monocacy, one must first review the circumstances that brought the two opposing forces together on July 9, 1864.

Lieutenant General Jubal Early had pulled the Second Corps of the Army of Northern Virginia out of the defenses of Richmond on June 13, and thus began the last great Confederate offensive of the war. Three years of hard campaigning, capped off by the intense fighting in the Wilderness, had reduced his command to 8,000 muskets and 24 pieces of artillery. Many regiments were little better than namesake organizations, but every man could be counted on to fight.

Moving by rail and on foot, Early arrived in the nick of time to prevent General David Hunter from capturing the vital Confederate supply base at Lynchburg, Virginia. Hunter escaped into West Virginia, but in doing so, took himself and his command out of the war for the rest of the summer.

Turning from the pursuit of Hunter, Early marched the length of the Shenandoah Valley, thus securing the year's harvest so desperately needed by the struggling Confederacy. Next, he forced the evacuation of Martinsburg and Harpers Ferry, and then as the two garrisons clung to each other atop Maryland Heights, he slipped across the Potomac, cleared the mountains, and collected his $200,000 bonus with the capture of Frederick, Maryland. Now, with an army of not more than 12,000 men, he was within a days march of the Federal capitol. With the defenses of Washington stripped of most of its men to feed Grant's war of attrition in Virginia, it was not unrealistic to contemplate one of two scenarios:

The first would be to lay seige to the capitol while the cavalry of McCausland and Johnson were sent to Southern Maryland to free the thousands of prisoners at Point Lookout. With this significant increase in manpower, Early would then hold the option of pressing the attack or returning to Virginia with more men than he had left with.

The second would be to attack, and if possible, capture a portion of Washington. Even if held for only a day, this would undoubtedly cause Grant to dispatch a large number of troops from the Petersburg area and give some relief to Lee's hard pressed army. Thus, the value of the days march cannot be overestimated.

For Major General Lew Wallace, the march had not been nearly as hard or as long. As commander of the Middle Department, his headquarters were in Baltimore. On learning of a Confederate advance working towards Harpers Ferry, he quickly mobilized those forces available to him. Working with the ever efficient president of the Baltimore and Ohio Railroad, John Garrett, Wallace's 2,500 men were sent by special trains from Baltimore to Monocacy Bridge, the western limit of his authority. In an effort to save Frederick from capture, he moved most of his troops to the west side of the city, and contested the advance of Johnson's brigade until he was warned of approaching Confederate infantry moving toward the Washington Road. Wallace pulled back to the east bank of the Monocacy River on the night of July 8, where he was joined by two brigades of veterans from the Sixth Corps. This brought the size of his little army up to about 6,000 men, many of which were 100-day volunteers. Confederate strength was overestimated at 20,000 to 30,000.

Wallace knew he had little chance to win against Early, but he had no choice except to stay and fight. By giving battle, he would force the enemy to show its strength. He would also cause Early to reveal his true objective — Baltimore, Washington, or a northward thrust into Pennsylvania. Finally, he would fight for time — a days march could determine the fate of the capitol.

In 1864, two major highways radiated from the southeast side of Frederick City, forming an upside down V. To the east , ran the Baltimore Pike which crossed the Monocacy River over a stone bridge known as Jug Bridge. To the south, ran the Washington Pike. It crossed the river on a covered wooden bridge just below the iron railroad bridge at Monocacy Junction. In order to impede Early's advance, Wallace had to cover all three of these structures, plus the fords, both above and below the highways.

Wallace believed that Early's main objective was Washington. Therefore, he placed Rickett's two brigades from the Sixth Corps on his left to cover the Washington Pike and the iron bridge. Further to the south, Clendenin's cavalry watched the lower fords and the far left flank of the Union line. His right flank was guarded by miscellaneous units that composed the First Separate Brigade, commanded by General Tyler. Midway between the railroad and the stone bridge, three companies of the Third Regiment Potomac Home Brigade were posted to watch Crum's Ford. Further up the river, Colonel A.L. Brown's mixed command of the Ohio National Guardsmen and the mounted infantry were ordered to hold Jug Bridge at all cost. On the west bank of the river between the railroad and the covered bridge, was a blockhouse. Wallace sent about 350 men across the river to occupy the blockhouse and form a skirmish line to cover the west end of the two bridges. Back on the east bank of the river was a 24-pound Howitzer in a small earthwork, supported by two 100-day regiments of Maryland troops — Wallace's only reserve. Finally, Alexander's battery of rifled guns was distributed evenly, with three guns on each flank.[38]

On the morning of July 8, 1864, Early's main interest was in the shortest route to the Federal capitol. He ordered Major General S.D. Ramseur to move his division out of Frederick along the Washington Pike, testing the defenses of the covered bridge. At the same time, Robert Rodes' division was sent against the stone bridge on the Union right.

Ramseur's first attack began at 9:30 a.m. Surprised by the heavy fire laid down by the Yankees on his side of the river, and the Howitzer on the other banks, he quickly pulled back.[39]

A mile or so downstream, McCausland's brigade of cavalry found a ford and crossed unobserved around 11 a.m. McCausland dismounted most of his men and sent the horse holders back across the river. Then he formed a line of battle and with flags flying, marched up river to find the enemy. What he found was a line of Union infantry lying behind a rail fence that delivered a murderous volley at short range, completely breaking his formation.[40] Regrouping near the Worthington's barn, McCausland advanced again at 2 p.m. This time, he moved to the right in order to flank the Yankees behind the fence separating the Worthington's and Thomas' farms. The movement was successful; the Union infantry fell back to their main line of defense along the Georgetown Road. At this point, Wallace observed the limited strength of McCausland's command and ordered a counter attack that drove the Confederates all the way back to their fording place at the river.[41]

While McCausland's troopers were engaged with Rickett's men on the left, Ramseur's division attacked the Union center again at noon. Fearing his forces west of the river would be overrun, Wallace pulled them back and ordered the blockhouse and covered bridge burned.[42] Unfortunately, no one communicated these instructions to the skirmish line operating outside of the blockhouse. As the hours passed, many of the men left behind retreated across the railroad bridge on their own initiative.

Lieutenant George E. Davis, Company D, Tenth Vermont Volunteers, was in charge of the skirmishers outside the blockhouse. Even after the bridge was burned, he and his company continued to contest the advance of Ramseur's men. A third Confederate attack

*Gen. Benjamin F. Butler*

*Gov. Thomas H. Hicks*

*Chief Justice R.B. Taney*

*John* Ex Parte *Merryman*

Erick F. Davis

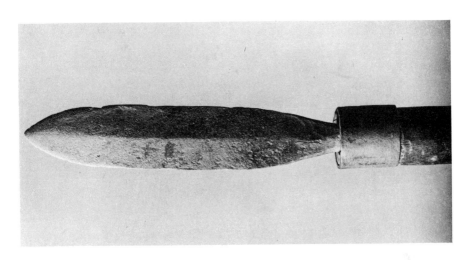

The Civil War has often been called the last romantic war or the first modern one. Nothing represents this concept more than two weapons manufactured by Ross Winans in 1861. (top) One of the pikes ordered by Marshal Kane. (bottom) The Winans Steam Gun. It's inventor claimed it could fire up to 500 rounds a minute.

WINANS STEAM GUN, CAPTURED BY COLONEL JONES ON THE WAY TO HARPER'S FERRY.—PHOTOGRAPHED BY WEAVER.

*Gov. Augustus W. Bradford*

*Gen. John A. Dix*

*Col. John R. Kenly*

*Judge Richard Carmichael*

Gen. Samuel Garland

Gen. Jesse Reno

Erick F. Davis

Gen. James J. Pettigrew

Gen. John D. Imboden

Erick F. Davis

113

# LIST OF DRAFTED MEN IN
## Somerset County.

BARREN CREEK.—Josephus Venables, w; Samuel Windsor, w; James S. Bedsworth, w; John H. Baily, w; Thomas Evans, w.

Per Cent.—Henry Thomas, w; Josiah S. Taylor, w; Wm W Gilliss, w; Azariah Sewell w; Jas. H. Philips, w.

QUANTICO.—James Church, col.; John W. Turpin, w.

Per Cent.—William Dashield, w; Wesley Gale, col.

TYASKIN.—Luther Waller, w; William Nutter, col.; Theodore P. Carter, w; John S. Jones, w; Zebediah Kelly, w; Henry C. Smith, w; Robert Layfield, col.; Franklin White, w.

Per Cent.—Isaac Speaker, w; Caleb R. Dashield, w, Gilbert Larmore, w; Henry Elzy, col.; John W. Turner, w; Alexander Messick, w; Emory Messick, w; Isaac F. Messick, col.

DAMES QUARTER.—John Wallace, w; Thomas Muir, w; Ephraim Dize, w; Charles Ennalls c; John B. Bozman, w; Nathaniel White, w; James Muir, w; John T. Parkinson, white.

Per Cent.—William McGrath, w; George Dryan, w; George Tyler, w: Edward Parks, w; James Bussels, w; George Barclay, w; Edward Phoebus, w; Edward White, w of S.

PRINCESS ANNE.—Arthur Wallace, colored; Francis Horsey; col.; Edwd. Hayman; col.; Gilbert Cox, white; John Stewart; col.; John White, col.; Ephraim Horsey, colored.

Per Cent.—Randal Hayman; w; Thomas Beauchamp w, Lewis Barns c, Geo. Milbourn col.John Bausman c, Wm. Pollet w, Isaac Horner, col.

BRINKLEY.—George Hayman; c; Benjamin Colburn, w; John Mitchell, w; James Moore, c; Edward Hall, c; Wiliam Shelton, w; William Adams, w.

Per Cent.—Isaac Marshall, c; Moses Howard· c; William Beauchamp, w; Washington Tull, w; Samuel Bevans, w; Godlife Fathier, w; Authur Lankford, w.

TRAPPE.—Alexander Murrell, w; Reuben Washboard, w; Samuel William, w; James Slemmons, c; Samuel Jones, w; Wesley Dove, w; Wesley Brewington, col.

Per Cent.—John T. Murray, c; Levin Packham, c; Samuel Horsey, c; William Cannon, w; William Townsend, w; William Smith, w; Emory Jones, w.

DUBLIN.—John Mariner, w; Joseph Pusey, w; George Adams, c; Thomas Dyke, w; James Coster, c.

Per cent.—Thomas Hemming, w; John Mills, w; Santa Anna Long, w; Hambleton Riggin, w; Wesley Parker, c.

SALISBURY.—James A. Parsons, white; Thos. Beauchamp, w.; John H. White, w.; Wm. J. Windsor, w.; Wm. J. Humphreys w.; Joshua Pinkett, col.; Elzy Hearn col.; Henry Leonard, col.; Jater Williams, col.; Noah Jenkins, white.

Per cent.—Thomas Philips, w.; Benjamin Dashiell, col.; Purnell Toadvine, w.; Rufus W. Trader, w.; Noah Baly, w.; Levin Johnson, col; John Laurenc, w.; Joseph Waller, w.; George Wood, c; James Owens, w.

HUNGARY NECK.—Horace Bounds, col; Peter Williams, w.

Per Cent.—Francis Hamlin, w; Isaac M. Austin, w.

POTATO NECK.—Robert Waters, c; Joshua Sudler, c; David Revel, w; John Jones, w; James Wilson, col; Abraham Quinn, col; Sutler Catlin, w.

Per Cent.—Riley Lander, w; Wm. E Hall c; Charles Howarth, w; George Ford, w; Joseph Hopkins. w; William S. Walker, w; Hance Ballard, w.

SMITH ISLAND.—John Dize, w; Benjamin Marsh, w; Solomon S. Evans.

Per Cent.—Solomon Evans, w; Walton Marsh, w; James Mister, w,

SHARPTOWN.—A. Qunton, c; Thomas Lowe, w; Wm. Dashield, (of T.) w; Hurst Boyce, c; James McGlotten, c; John T. Philips, w.

Per Cent.—Wm. H Cooper, w; Benjamin S. Bradly, w; Elijah Philips, w; Peter Taylor, w; George H. River, w; Isaac J. Baily, white.

LAWSONS.—George Bell, c; Jacob B. Cullen, w; A. D. Dougherty, w; Severn Cullen, w; Andrew F. Riggin, w; William Sterling, w.

Per Cent.—Levi S. Dougherty, w; Lewis Burton, c; Alexander Nelson, w; Edward Ward, w; Elijah Summers, w; John G. Handy, c.

TANGIERS.—Noah S. Rider, w; Jacob W. Webster, w; Benj. J. N. Jones, w; John Parks, c; James T. Daniel w.

Per Cent.—William Thomas, w; Robert Bradshaw, w; Isaac W. Hickman, w; Elijah Williams, w; Herod Armstrong, c.

*Gen. Jubal A. Early*

*Gen. Lew Wallace*

*Gen. Bradley T. Johnson*

*Major Harry Gilmor*

*John Wilkes Booth and his conspirators*

*Camp Parole near Annapolis*

*Commander Foxhall Parker*

*Monument to Ladd and Whitney*

came at 3 p.m. Fearing his men would be cut off, Davis maneuvered them back toward the railroad bridge, leading them over the iron structure to the safety of the Union lines. For his gallant service in the engagement, he was awarded the Congressional Medal of Honor.[43]

As soon as Early realized that McCausland had found a place to cross the river, he ordered Gordon's division to swing around behind the Confederate right, cross the river, and deliver a flank attack in the same general area where the dismounted cavalry had been fighting. Unfortunately for the Confederates, their maneuvers did not go undetected. Rickett's changed front and faced the oncoming Rebel's from behind fence rails and in sunken roadbeds. Gordon sent in first, Evans' brigade, then York's and finally Terry's. The fighting between these two veteran organizations was intense and deadly. General Clement Evans was wounded and a number of line officers were killed. General Gordon's horse was shot from under him, but he remained unharmed. At one point, where the fighting crossed a stream, the water flowed red for over 100 yards with the blood of soldiers from both sides.[44] By 4 p.m., Rickett's two brigades had been pushed across the Washington Pike and the railroad. This allowed Ramseur's men to pour across the river and join in the final attack.[45]

As the veterans of the Sixth Corps slowly backed towards their escape route on the Baltimore Pike, Tyler committed his last reserves to the holding of the Jug Bridge. His position was soon overrun and Union resistance was disintegrated. Hundreds of Wallace's men, including Tyler, escaped through the woods. It took several days to regain their command. The balance of the Union army retreated toward New Market on the road to Baltimore.[46]

In his after action report, Wallace stated his losses as 1,294 total.[47] Early estimated his losses at 600 to 700.[48] This is probably low, since Gordon had reported 698 casualties in his division alone.[49]

Wallace had done all he could with his limited resources. Although driven from the field, he could take solace in the fact that after the day long battle, Early's Rebels were still no closer to Washington.


URBANA

Clendenin was patrolling the fords on the Union left with various squadrons and companies of the Eighth Illinois Cavalry. At

118

the same time, Major Wells was at Urbana with 50 men patrolling the Buckeystown Road. When McCausland's cavalry forced its way across Monocacy River, Clendenin and a number of his men were cut off, but managed to escape capture, reforming on the Georgetown Pike near Monocacy Junction. They held this position until Gordon's infantry division made its attack later in the day.

Pursued by Confederate cavalry, Clendenin retreated to Urbana where he joined forces with Major Wells. Here, they repelled a charge of the Seventeenth Virginia and captured the regiment's colonel, color bearer and flag. Seeing a much larger force of enemy cavalry approaching the town, Clendenin sent out a strong skirmish line to give the impression that his force was much larger than what he actually had. The plan worked. McCausland's troopers dismounted and advanced cautiously on foot.

Clendenin took this opportunity to recall his skirmishes and withdrew to Monrovia where he found several wagonloads of wounded and straggling infantry making their way east. He fell in with this column and covered its rear all the way to Ellicott Mills. His losses for the day were, one officer killed and five men wounded. Companies D and I were cut off earlier in the day when Gordon's division crossed the river and were forced to retreat toward Washington.[50]

# 10 FREDERICK

Union cavalry led by Lieutenant William Blakely, reoccupied Frederick City on July 10 and skirmished with Early's rear guard. One man from the Twenty-First New York Cavalry was captured.[51] During the next two days, Medical Inspector G.K. Johnson reported burying 121 Federal soldiers. He also found 189 Union soldiers in the hospital there, and 15 at New Market. The Confederates left 405 wounded men behind in the Frederick hospital.[52]

## ROCKVILLE

Major William H. Fry was placed in command of a Provisional Cavalry Regiment and ordered to scout the area toward Frederick. He left the fortifications of Washington on the morning of the 9th and camped that night at Falls Run. He then proceeded to Rockville, where he met Wells and the men of the Eighth Illinois Cavalry that had been cut off from their regiment during the fighting at Monocacy. Wells joined Fry's expedition and the two units continued along the Frederick Road until they encountered a Rebel skirmish line at the village of Gerrardsville. Beyond the skirmish line was a column of Confederate cavalry moving in their direction. Fry ordered an about face and marched back through Rockville, continuing one mile beyond to a hill behind the town. Here he dismounted his men and held his ground until the Southerners brought up a battery and shelled him out of position.[53]

**11** The District of Columbia Militia was called into the service of the United States Army.

Major General E.O.C. Ord was assigned to command the Eighth Army Corps and all troops in the Middle Department.[54]

MUDDY BRANCH

Mosby crossed the Potomac River at Conrad's Ferry. Moving in the direction of Poolesville, he came across some blockhouses and burned them. He continued his march until he reached Muddy Branch, where he found a deserted camp of the Eighth Illinois Cavalry, containing tents, bags of oats and other camp equipment. Mosby ordered his men to burn the camp and a large blockhouse nearby. Then he and his men recrossed the river taking 30 head of cattle from the camp.[55]

**11-13** FORT STEVENS
When word reached government officials in Washington of Wallace's defeat at Monocacy, the greatest fear for the safety of the president and the capitol prevailed. Every unassigned soldier or unit was rushed to the city's defense. Quartermaster General of the Army Montgomery C. Meigs, organized his clerks and bookkeepers into a division of 2,700 strong.[56] The quest for manpower was best summed up by the following letter from General

120

Helleck to an officer who had offered his services:

Washington, D.C.
July 11, 1864

Brig.-Gen. J.B. West
Fifth Avenue Hotel, New York

We have five times as many generals here as we want, but are greatly in need of privates. Anyone volunteering in that capacity will be thankfully received.

H.W. Halleck
Major-General and Chief of Staff[57]

On the 10th, Early pulled his bone tired army together and set out on a 40 mile trek to capture the capitol of the United States. That night, his men slept in Rockville. As Early's men marched through the dust and heat of the Maryland summer, two divisions of the Sixth Corps were sailing north from City Point, Virginia. Grant had dispatched 11,000 men under Major General H.G. Wright to the relief of Washington.[58]

Rode's division led the advance on the 11th, but at a slower pace due to the heat. Marching along the Seventh Street Pike, they appeared in front of Fort Stevens around 11 a.m. Rode's men deployed for action and began to push the Union pickets back in front of Fort Stevens and Fort DeRussy.

Early made his headquarters at Silver Springs, the home of Montgomery Blair, Postmaster General of the United States. As his army continued to arrive throughout the day, he took the opportunity to study the enemy's defenses. "They consist of a circle of inclosed forts, connected by breastworks, with ditches, palisades, and abatis in front, and every approach swept by an across-fire of artillery. . ." The forts were strong, but lightly manned and Early made the decision to attack as soon as possible, despite the fact his infantry force did not exceed 10,000 men.[59] By 4 p.m. the Confederates had pushed to within 100 yards of Fort Stevens. Sharpshooters occupied a number of houses and outbuildings in the area, drawing fire from the big guns in both forts.[60]

Before Early could organize an all out attack, he observed reinforcements filing into Fort Stevens. Other blue-clad figures were seen advancing to support the badly sagging skirmish line in front of the works. Wheaton's brigade of the Sixth Corps had disembarked in Washington at noon, arriving at the fort around 4 p.m.

General Wright ordered a force of 500 men to relieve the contingent of Veteran Reserve Corps, War Department clerks and citizen volunteers outside the fort and to regain the line lost in the afternoon. This was accomplished by 7 p.m.[61] Throughout the night, boats continued to arrive at the dock in Washington, so that by the morning of the 12th, the safety of the capitol was insured.

Early called a halt to the offensive operations after the attack on his skirmish line. He was not about to throw this army against an unknown enemy in the dark. Johnson had warned him about the Sixth Corps and a rumor was afloat that the Nineteenth Corps was returning from Louisiana as well. Still, this limited success could have been the result of last minute shifts of the existing garrison. Early held a council of war and told his generals that if things were unchanged in the morning, he would order an all out assault.[62]

Tuesday morning revealed the presence of thousands of fresh troops in the Union fortification. There would be no grand assault on the capitol. There was no retreat either. Early's decision to hold his position as long as possible was a sound one. Johnson's cavalry had not yet returned from Southern Maryland. A premature withdraw would have left him cut off behind enemy lines. The Union war machine was still psychologically on the defensive and his presence near the enemy's capitol would bear a positive effect on Southern morale. Finally, every day spent north of the Potomac was that much less a strain on the Virginia countryside.

July 12 passed in relative quiet until 6 p.m., when batteries from both Fort Stevens and Fort Slocum commenced a concentrated fire on a section of the Confederate line in front of Fort Stevens. From the Carbury and River's homes and two wooded hills in this area, Rebel sharpshooters were picking off Union soldiers, both on the skirmish line and in the fort.[63] One man had been struck as he stood by the side of Abraham Lincoln. Old Abe had climbed the fort's parapet to view the pending battle, unmindful of his own personal danger. A young infantry officer, unaware that the civilian presenting such an excellent target to the enemy's sharpshooters was the president of the United States, yelled, "Get down, you fool." The officer was Captain Oliver Wendell Holmes, Jr.[64]

After the 36th shot had been discharged from Fort Stevens, the barrage stopped and Wheaton's brigade, reinforced with three regiments from the Third Brigade, launched a surprise attack. Confederate resistance was stronger than anticipated and the balance of the Third Brigade was committed before objectives could be gained. Brigadier General Frank Wheaton, acting commander of the Second Division, reported 204 men killed or wounded in the twilight encounter that did not end until 10 p.m.[65]

As soon as the Union advance was checked, Early began issuing orders for the return of his army to Virginia. Henry Kyd Douglas, a Marylander on Early's staff, was summoned to a meeting on the night of the 12th, attended by Generals Breckinridge and Gordon. In recounting his wartime experiences, Douglas told of the following interviews:

> "Major, we haven't taken Washington, but we've scared Abe Lincoln like hell!"
>
> "Yes General," I replied, "but this afternoon when that Yankee line moved out against us, I think some other people were scared blue as hell's brimstone!"
>
> How about that, General," said Breckinridge with a laugh. "That's true," piped General Early, "but it won't appear in history."
>
> "Then he informed me that we were about to leave; that he had directed a detail of two hundred men, with proper officers to be left on the picket line; that I should remain with them and keep them there until after midnight, unless driven in or ordered away before that time, and then march as a rear guard until cavalry fell in behind me."

Shortly after midnight, Douglas called for his men and began to march toward the Potomac. A short time later, someone acting without orders set fire to the Blair mansion. The fire illuminated the sky, giving notice to the Confederate's withdraw.[66]

# 9-13 THE JOHNSON-GILMOR RAIDS

During Jubal Early's operations against Washington, the cavalry brigade of Bradley T. Johnson operated independently of the main Confederate force. Its mission touched the outer limits of reality and had it been completely successful, it would have been the most spectacular cavalry operation of the Civil War.

Following the death of General William E. "Grumble" Jones at the battle of Piedmont, General Johnson was promoted to the rank of Brigadier General and given command of Jones' old brigade of approximately 1,500 men. Transferred along with Johnson was the First Maryland Cavalry and the Second Maryland Battalion under the command of Major Harry Gilmor. On the night of July 8, 1864, Johnson received his orders from General Early and was given as much background information as the commanding officer possessed.

The next day, Johnson was to position his brigade on the left flank of the Confederate army. As soon as he was certain of a Southern victory, he was to strike out to the north of Baltimore, cutting rail and telegraph lines running into the city. Then he was to reverse his march, moving through Southern Maryland to Point Lookout Prison where he would effect the release of 10 to 12 thousand Confederate prisoners held there.[67] His attack was to be supported by the *C.S.S. Tallahassee*, commanded by John Taylor Wood, C.S.N. After releasing the prisoners, Johnson was to march them to Washington, D.C. where he was to join Early in an attack on the Union capitol. Finally, Early told Johnson that he would have to reach Point Lookout by July 12. This meant an incredible march of 300 miles through enemy territory in only 96 hours with no extra time for fighting, sleeping, or destroying railroad property.[68]

Unknown to Early, Commander Wood sailed from Wilmington, North Carolina on July 10. On board his steamer were several field pieces, 20,000 weapons to be issued to the liberated soldiers and a detachment of Confederate marines commanded by General G.W. Custis Lee. As the steamer waited in an inlet for a favorable tide to put to sea on, the expedition was cancelled by President Jefferson Davis. Davis believed the plans had been discovered by the enemy, and that the Northern forces were waiting to capture the *Tallahassee*.[69]

As soon as it became evident that Early would win the day at

Monocacy, Johnson struck off in the direction of New Windsor where the brigade stopped and forced local shopkeepers to open their stores and sell their wares for Confederate money. Before leaving, the raiders set fire to the railroad station and a bridge on the Western Maryland line. The fires were extinguished, however, before serious damage occurred.[70]

While Johnson held New Windsor, Gilmor and 20 men rode ahead to Westminster where they occupied the town and cut the telegraph lines.[71] From Westminster, Johnson moved to Cockeysville where he arrived on the 10th, with Gilmor's men acting as an advance guard. After setting fire to the bridges of the Northern Central Railroad, Gilmor was ordered to take a small force and burn the bridge of the Philadelphia, Wilmington and Baltimore Railroad where it crossed the Gunpowder River further downstream. Gilmor was also instructed to disrupt communications as much as possible between Baltimore and the North.

On the 11th, Johnson went to the estate of John "Ex Parte" Merryman, known as Hayfields, for lunch. Merryman had been one of the bridge burners in April of 1861. From Cockeysville, the main Confederate force moved through Green Spring Valley to within a few miles of Baltimore City. That night, Johnson rested his command for a few hours at the home of John N. Carroll, called The Caves. Around midnight, Johnson received word of the expected arrival of the Sixth and Nineteenth Corps. He quickly dispatched a courier to Early with this information.[72]

Breaking camp before sun up on the 12th, the Confederates rode through Owings Mills, just as the employees of Painters Mill were loading a boxcar with chests of ice cream for sale in Baltimore. Johnson allowed his men to help themselves to the "frozen vittles." A number of Rebels were from Southwest Virginia and had never seen ice cream before. With the special enthusiasm of hungry soldiers, they pressed every available cup, pail and tin cup into service. Even a few hats were used, as nearly the entire brigade partook of this rarest of all treats.[73] This may, in fact, have been the largest ice cream social held in either army during the Civil War.

Johnson's last action while north of Baltimore was to send a detail of men from the First Maryland Cavalry under Lieutenant Henry Blackistone to the home of Governor Augustus W. Bradford on North Charles Street. The Bradford residence was burned in

125

retaliation for the destruction of Governor John Letcher's home in Lexington, Virginia by General Hunter.[74] Leaving Harry Gilmor to operate independently in Baltimore County, Johnson began to move in the direction of Point Lookout. He crossed the Baltimore and Ohio Railroad above Woodstock and stopped for lunch at Doughoregan Manor, the home of John Lee Carroll, a post war governor of Maryland. Riding through parts of Howard and Montgomery Counties, he did not reach Triadelphia until after 9 p.m., where the horses were unsaddled and a few hours sleep granted to both man and beast.[75]

When Johnson broke camp on the morning of the 13th, he headed toward Laurel, the point at which he intended to cross the Washington branch of the Baltimore and Ohio Railroad. Enroute, he learned of the presence of a large force of Federal infantry and changed course for Beltsville, which was six miles closer to Washington.

At Beltsville, the Confederates captured a construction crew and camp train belonging to the Baltimore and Ohio Railroad. Seven cars, along with other railroad property, were burned. Two gondolas and 11 ballast cars found on a siding were also burned and eight telegraph poles were cut down.[77]

A force of 500 Union cavalry was set out from the fortifications of Washington to investigate the cause of the smoke seen rising from the burned trains. From the top of a hill, Johnson and two scouts from the First Maryland Cavalry, watched the advancing enemy pull down fences and deploy his skirmishers. Johnson ordered the Baltimore Light Artillery to go into battery and shell the Yankee horsemen. The Union advance quickly changed direction and sought the shelter of the capitol. Captain Wilson C. Nicholas led squadrons E and F of the First Maryland after the fleeing Yankee's in an unsuccessful attempt to gobble up a few stragglers.[78]

Before leaving Beltsville, the Confederates rounded up several hundred government mules, intending to use them in mounting some of the released prisoners. Johnson had just put his column in motion on the Marlboro Road, when a courier arrived with orders from Early to abandon the Point Lookout operation and rejoin the main army at Silver Springs. Changing direction, the Confederates followed the Washington Turnpike as far as the Agricultural College, where they had a brief skirmish with a Federal cavalry patrol. At this point,

126

Johnson ordered George W. Booth, Adjutant of the First Maryland to lead the advance with a number of men who had been residents of the area before the war. Each crossroad along their route was picketed until the column passed. Under the cover of darkness, Johnson's brigade of 1200 to 1300 men, with artillery, wagons and the herd of captured mules, scrapped the outer defenses of the Federal capitol as it made its way to rejoin Early. Had this march been attempted in daylight, the column would have been shelled to pieces by the heavy guns within the Union forts. Booth arrived at Early's headquarters shortly after 9 p.m., and found the army already in retreat. General Johnson did not report to Early until after midnight, which indicates he must have been with the rear-most unit of his command.[79]

It will be remembered that Johnson dispatched Harry Gilmor on the 10th to cut the railroad north of Baltimore. Gilmor left Cockeysville at noon with 130 men of the First and Second Maryland Cavalry. Enroute, he stopped at his boyhood home, Glen Ellen, for a short visit with his family. The next day, he marched across Bel Air and Harford Roads, cutting telegraph lines whenever the opportunity presented itself. At the home of Ishmael Day, an advanced guard of two men stopped and ordered Day to haul down a National flag he had flying in front of his house, Day refused and Ordnance Sergeant Eugene Fields dismounted to do it himself. Day grabbed a shotgun and fatally wounded Fields. He then escaped into the woods. When Gilmor's men came up, they vented their anger by burning Day's house and barn.

At Magnolia Station, Gilmor captured a train from Baltimore. Among its passengers were a number of Union officers and Major General William B. Franklin. The passengers and their baggage were unloaded. Then the train was burned after it was learned that the engineer had disabled the locomotive and fled. Gilmor checked the schedule and settled down to wait for the next train, which was due in about one hour.[80]

By now, Union authorities were well aware of the Confederate advance into Northern Maryland. At Wilmington, Delaware, Major Henry B. Judd, the post commander, began mobilizing forces to counter the Rebel invasion. One hundred convalescents and men of the Veteran Reserve Corps were sent under the command of Lieutenant James Lewis to Havre de Grace, to protect the ferry boat and railroad property there. After failing to raise any 100-day volunteer units, Judd reduced the term of service to 30-days, eventually fielding an entire regiment, the Seventh Delaware Infantry.

Finding all means of communication with Baltimore severed, Judd moved to Havre de Grace and assumed command of the town and all troops there, including a detachment of sailors and marines serving a naval battery under Captain Thomas C. Harris, U.S.N. Judd's force was augmented by a company of volunteer cavalry and a section of Pennsylvania artillery under Captain Stanislaus Motkowski. Scouts were sent to the Conowingo Bridge on the Susquehanna River, where preparations were made to either defend or destroy the bridge, as circumstances dictated. All vessels capable of passing through the Chesapeake and Delaware Canal were seized and sent to Perryville for the transportation of troops to Baltimore.

As soon as the first 50 men volunteered for 30-days service, they were formed into a company under Captain Thomas Hugh Stirling and sent to reinforce a detachment guarding the Philadelphia, Wilmington and Baltimore Railroad Bridge over the Gunpowder River.[81] At the bridge, Lieutenant Robert Price, with 32 men of Company F, One Hundred and Ninth Regiment, Ohio National Guard, had been standing guard day and night. Stirling's men arrived at 3 o'clock in the morning on the 10th, and took charge of the eastern end of the bridge.[82]

After capturing the second train, Gilmor ordered Captain Bailey to move up his sharpshooters and open fire. Then he set fire to the train and backed it on to the bridge. One of Stirling's men was wounded and a few were forced to jump into the river to avoid the burning cars.[83] The captain led the rest of his men back towards the center of the bridge where they met Lieutenant Price and his detachment. Acting quickly, they succeeded in uncoupling two cars and pushing them to safety. The draw span was destroyed as the burning cars crashed through to the river below. During the entire affair, the steamer *Juniata* lay at anchor 300 yards downstream and offered no assistance in the bridge's defense.[84]

Following the action at the bridge, Gilmor paroled most of his officers captured on the two trains. Loading General Franklin and a few others into a carriage, he turned his command south, heading toward Baltimore. Learning from a citizen of the defensive measures taken in the city, Gilmor changed course for Towsontown.

That night, Gilmor entered Towsontown at the head of his command and stopped for a drink at the Ady's Hotel. Then learning of an advance by Union cavalry from Baltimore, he sent off his prisoners with a detachment of 10 men. Lieutenant William H. Kemp was ordered to take 15 men from Company C and charge the enemy's advance guard, while Gilmor laid a trap with the rest of his force.

The enemy turned out to be about 75 mounted volunteers under the command of Captain Haverstick. The skittish volunteers were quickly driven off and pursued as far as Govanstown by some of Gilmor's men.

By now, most of Gilmor's men were riding in their sleep, having had little food or rest for nearly 48 hours. Passing through Green Spring Valley, they arrived at the home of Mr. Craddock where Captain Nickolas Owings had been ordered to wait with the prisoners. Upon arriving, Gilmor found the guards asleep and General Franklin and the other prisoners gone. At this point, Gilmor allowed his men to eat and feed their horses and get a few hours of sleep. The rest of the day of July 12 was spent near Pikesville. Crossing through the center of the state, they did not reach General Johnson's headquarters near Poolesville until the morning of the 14th.[85]

# 13 ROCKVILLE

When Bradley Johnson's brigade, less Gilmor's detachment, rejoined Early's army on the night of the 12th, Johnson was ordered to take charge of the rear guard, following up the infantry and wagon trains with his and Jackson's cavalry brigades. At Rockville, the Second Massachusetts Cavalry, led by Colonel Charles R. Lowell, engaged Jackson's men around mid-day. Johnson ordered a counter attack by a squadron of the First Maryland Cavalry which cleared the town of Yankees. In the charge, the horses of Captain Wilson C. Nicholas and Lieutenant Thomas Green were killed and the two officers were captured by the Union forces. When Johnson learned of the two men's fate, he immediately ordered a second charge and succeeded in recapturing Lieutenant Green. Captain Nicholas had been remounted and taken off the field before help could arrive.[86]

In following up the Confederate retreat, the usual number of stragglers and wounded were picked up. One Johnny Reb had exceptionally poor luck. He was found lying unconscious with his skull crushed and a huge shell fragment laying nearby. He had apparently been struck by one of the 11-inch guns in Fort Stevens, which was three miles away! Taken to Lincoln Hospital in an ambulance train, he lived until July 17.[87]

**13-14** THE SOUTH RIVER EXPEDITION

In order to protect the Union army's camps and hospitals near Annapolis from Confederate raiders, Lieutenant Commander Braine of the *U.S.S. Vicksburg* sent a boat expedition to destroy all means of crossing the South River. The expedition was commanded by Acting Ensign Francis C. Osborn.[88]

**14** POOLESVILLE

Having marched all night, Johnson's brigade took up a defensive position at Poolesville, while Early's army crossed the Potomac at Edward's, White's and Noland's Ferries.[89] Throughout the morning, wagons, prisoners, and hundreds of captured cattle and horses splashed across the river as Johnson's troopers skirmished with the Union cavalry. Late in the afternoon, blue-clad infantry were seen deploying in numbers too great for Johnson's men to contend with. The guns of the Baltimore Light Artillery kept up steady fire until the last wagon had crossed the river. Then Johnson broke off the action and returned to Virginia as the sun went down on the last major Confederate invasion of the North.[90]

Early's Valley Campaign of 1864 was a combination of success and failure. His greatest single accomplishment was to clear the Shenandoah Valley of Union troops and allow most of the summers crops to be harvested for the Confederacy. He won a battle he did not wish to fight at Monocacy, and lost the foot race to the Federal capitol. His paper-thin seige of Washington caused the diversion of two army corps from Grant's Army, but the destruction wrought by the Johnson-Gilmor raid was quickly repaired and hardly worth the gamble. Had the release of the prisoners at Point Lookout been effected, the sadly depleted Valley Army would have been

130

reconstituted overnight. This would have greatly enhanced Early's ability to defend the valley and possibly save it from Sheridan's torch. Had Early been able to keep his army together through the winter, it is not inconceivable that Richmond would have fallen before Sheridan could have gained a major victory, and this is where the greatest criticism lies.

Early ordered Johnson to cover his left flank on July 9, and not to start his operation until the battle was clearly won. Then he was to ride north of Baltimore, burn a few bridges and then circle the city, so he could move south and arrive at Point Lookout by the night of the 12th, a ride of several hundred miles. With 10,000 Confederate prisoners at stake, it would have made more sense to send only Gilmor, with the combined Maryland commands and one or two pieces of artillery on a diversion north of the city and position the rest of Johnson's brigade behind the Confederate right flank. Johnson was from the area and had to know that there was little strategic importance between Frederick and Laurel. Therefore, there was little chance in colliding with a major Union force or garrison. Furthermore, most of the damages inflicted on the ride north of Baltimore was done by Gilmor's command. The remainder of the brigade was for the most part, unemployed until it struck the railroad at Beltsville.

Had Johnson's raid been launched from the south instead of the north side of Frederick after the battle on the 9th, he would have had ample time to reach Point Lookout by the 12th. The fact that the naval expedition never materialized is irrelevant, since neither Early or Johnson knew this until after the raid. With or without the gunboat, Johnson would have had an opportunity to test the defense of the prison. What effect a brigade of veteran cavalry and a commanding officer with a vivid imagination could have on a garrison of green troops can only be imagined.


## 25  WILLIAMSPORT

Following his campaign against Washington, Early attempted to keep his exhausted army as active as possible. He struck the Union forces under General George Crook at Winchester, Virginia on July 24. Crook's force was routed and thousands of Yankees streamed through Martinsburg on their way to safety in Maryland. The Union commander managed to keep most of his infantry units intact, maneuvering them north, where they crossed the Potomac River at Williamsport on the 25th.

After moving through Williamsport, Union cavalry assigned to rear guard duty, turned about and formed a battle line on the outskirts of town. When the pursuing enemy cavalry entered the town, they charged and drove them back across the river, taking a few Rebel prisoners in the process.[91]

## 26 WILLIAMSPORT

Following the engagement on the 25th, detachments from Averell's Union cavalry division guarded the river crossings from Hancock to Dam Number 4. General Averell took the balance of his command to Hagerstown. On the 26th a force of Confederate cavalry, estimated at 400 strong, crossed the river and attacked Averell's pickets at Williamsport. They recrossed the river the next day at Little Georgetown when approached by Union reinforcements.[92]

## 29 CLEAR SPRINGS

General Bradley T. Johnson's brigade of cavalry crossed the Potomac River at dawn, forcing the Union pickets back to Clear Springs. At this point, Colonel Harry Gilmor led the First Maryland Regiment and Second Maryland Battalion in a charge that cleared the town and drove the Union troops toward Hagerstown.[93]

The Union force consisted of 44 men and one officer from the Permanent Company at Carlisle Barracks. Under the command of First Lieutenant H.T. McLean, Sixth United States Cavalry, they had been detailed to watch McCoy's Ferry, Clear Springs, and Cherry Run. After the attack by Johnson's Confederates, they fought a delaying action as they retreated back into Pennsylvania.[94]

### DAM NUMBER 4

Captain William L. Atkinson, Company I, Cole's Maryland Cavalry, sent a detachment under Lieutenant Alexander M. Briscoe to cover up the ford at Dam Number 4. Briscoe was ordered to dispute the Confederate advance for as long as possible and to send regular reports on enemy troop movements. He was soon joined by two companies of the Tenth West Virginia Cavalry and some of the Twelfth Pennsylvania, all of which came under his command.

Throughout the day, enemy troops gathered to force a crossing at the dam. When a Southern officer attempted to lead a company of cavalry in a charge across the river, Lieutenant Briscoe shot him out of the saddle. His body splashed into the water and floated downstream as Yankee troopers opened fire and drove the Rebel cavalry back to the Virginia shore. Then Briscoe, ordering his men to mount up, withdrew with his detachment to Hagerstown.

## HAGERSTOWN

At Hagerstown, Major Robert Mooney, and four companies of Cole's Cavalry, aided by Provost Marshal Captain Limmerman, fought the Confederate advance through the town, street by street for three hours. After being forced out of Hagerstown, Mooney retreated to Greencastle, Pennsylvania. Several men from Cole's cavalry were killed, wounded or captured. Lieutenant Briscoe was captured when his horse was shot and fell on him, dislocating his hip. Adjutant O.A. Horner's horse was also killed.[95]

## 30 EMMITSBURG

Captain R.M. Evans of the Philadelphia City Scouts reported his pickets driven in by "200 Rebels." [96]

## MOUTH OF MONOCACY

Confederate cavalry from Mosby's Forty-Third Virginia Battalion, crossed the Potomac River at Cheek's Ford and attacked a Union picket of the Eighth Illinois Cavalry. Lieutenant DeLaney and three men were wounded, and two others killed. The Confederates also captured 25 horses and six or eight men.[97] They then proceeded to Adamstown, where they cut the telegraph lines and chopped down several telegraph poles. Leaving there, they set out to capture Federal picket posts at the mouth of the Monocacy River. Lieutenant Harry Hatcher led 25 men in a swing behind the enemy position. Lieutenant Nelson with the remainder of Companies A and D, moved along the river and launched a frontal attack. One of Nelson's men was shot in the head and killed. A second man was wounded and a number of horses were killed before Hatcher's men took the enemy position from the rear.

The Eighth Illinois Cavalry lost four men killed and 22 prisoners, along with a number of horses. After collecting their booty, Mosby's men returned to Virginia.[98]

## 31 HANCOCK

After the burning of Chambersburg, Pennsylvania, McCausland led his cavalry to Hancock where he demanded a ransom of $30,000 and 5,000 cook rations. General Bradley T. Johnson, one of McCausland's brigade commanders, argued that the population of only 700 could not possibly produce that much food or money. Fortunately for the citizens of Hancock, the issue was settled when Union cavalry from Brigadier General W.W. Averell's division approached. McCausland set off toward Cumberland while Johnson's command skirmished with the Union cavalry in a rear guard action before joining McCausland.[99]

# AUGUST 1864

Following his return to Virginia, General Early was instructed by Lee to keep the Army of the Shenandoah active in order to divert as many Union troops as possible away from the seige lines of Petersburg. To this end, Early sent the cavalry brigades of McCausland and Johnson across the Potomac for one, final raid into Pennsylvania.

Arriving at Chambersburg on July 30th, McCausland demanded a ransom of $100,000 in gold or $500,000 in currency. Failure to meet the demand would result in the destruction of the town. The townspeople could not be made to realize that the threat was real. When the time for payment had passed, Chambersburg was burned to the ground in retaliation for similar acts of destruction inflicted upon the citizens of Virginia by the Union Army.

Before returning to Virginia, McCausland attempted to capture Cumberland, but was driven off and crossed the Potomac River at Old Town the next day. A few days later, Averell's cavalry caught the Rebels in camp along the South Fork of the Potomac and badly routed McCausland's command, taking over 400 prisoners and two guns of the Baltimore Light Artillery.

The fruits of the Chambersburg Raid were all evil for the Confederacy. Grant transferred General Phillip H. Sheridan and two divisions of cavalry from the Army of the Potomac. Sheridan was ordered to knock Early and the Shenandoah Valley out of the war for good. As a result of the losses sustained by McCausland at South Fork, Early had only a limited number of cavalry to counter this new threat.

# 1 FLINTSTONE CREEK

Dyer's, *A Compendium of the War of the Rebellion,* Volume II, page 764, sites an action involving the Eleventh West Virginia Infantry.

## FLOCK'S MILL [CUMBERLAND]

With Confederate cavalry roaming unchecked through Western Maryland for the second time in as many months, General B.F. Kelly set about to defend the vital railroad property and government supply depot at Cumberland. At his disposal were three regiments of the Ohio National Guard, four companies of the Eleventh, and one company of the Sixth West Virginia Infantry regiments. Kelly also had two sections of Battery L, First Illinois Light Artillery; one section from Battery B, Maryland Light Artillery; and several hundred stragglers from the battle at Winchester on July 24th.

On August 1, Lieutenant T.W. Kelly led a squad of cavalry down the Baltimore Pike. His orders were to locate and then impede the Confederate advance. At noon, he sent a report to General Kelly stating that McCausland's command was 12 miles from the city. General Kelly immediately ordered Colonel Caleb Marker to take his One Hundred and Fifty-Sixth Ohio National Guards and Major J.L. Simpson's four companies of West Virginia Infantry to occupy the high ground two miles east of Cumberland where the Baltimore Pike crossed Evett's Creek. Marker's infantry was supported by one section of Battery L under Lieutenant John McAfee. The balance of the Federal troops occupied the fortification around Cumberland.

At 3:00 p.m., Confederate cavalry began crossing Evett's Creek. Marker opened fire with both cannon and musket, driving the surprised Rebels back across the bridge. McCausland's men took cover behind the bridge, and in Flock's mill, house and barn.[100]

135

Rebel sharpshooters attempted to drive off the Yankee gunners. Private Thomas Breen of Battery L was struck in the right eye by a musket ball. The ball passed downward through the bones in his face and lodged in his throat. Breen was able to cough out the musket ball, thus continuing to breathe. He was taken to the hospital in Cumberland where he remained until February 20, 1865. On that day, he was discharged blind in one eye, but still very much alive.[101]

McCausland sent forward reinforcements and opened on the Union position with four pieces of artillery. The battle lasted until after dark. Aware of Averell's cavalry somewhere near Hancock, and uncertain of the strength of Kelly's garrison at Cumberland, McCausland withdrew his forces under the cover of darkness. Kelly reported finding eight dead and 30 wounded Confederates near Flock's Mill the following day.[102]

## 2  OLD TOWN

Forced to abandon his raid on Cumberland, General McCausland ordered Johnson's brigade to march south on the night of August 1 and to secure a crossing over the Potomac. When the Confederates arrived at Old Town the next morning, they found the canal bridges burned, with Union troops in position on a hill between the canal and the river. Johnson immediately ordered the Eighth Virginia Regiment and the Twenty-Seventh Virginia Battalion to attack the hill, while the rest of his men crossed the canal on a hastily built bridge. At the same time, two guns from the Baltimore Light Artillery shelled the Federal position.[103]

Seeing the hordes of Rebel cavalry descending on his position, Colonel Israel Stough led his One Hundred and Fifty-Third Ohio National Guard across the river to Green Spring Depot, West Virginia. Stough and about 80 men took shelter in a blockhouse, while the rest of his command climbed back on the train that had brought them down from Cumberland and moved out of harms way. Supporting the Ohio troops was an armored train. The train consisted of iron-clad railroad batteries containing three guns each, and four musket proof boxcars with loop holes for riflemen. Manning the train was a detachment from Company K of the Second Regiment Potomac Home Brigade under Captain Peter B. Petrie.[104]

The treeline prevented Johnson's artillery from coming to bear on the blockhouse. A position was soon found, however, from which one gun of the Baltimore Light Artillery could fire on the train. Gunner George McElwee took careful aim and sent his first shot through the boiler of the locomotive. His second shot entered the port hole of one of the battery cars, dismounting a cannon. A third round landed in the railbed, showering the Union infantry with rocks and shrapnel. With the engine disabled, Petrie's men were sitting ducks. Leaping from the rail cars, they fled into the woods and left the Ohio Guardsmen to take care of themselves.[105] General Johnson then demanded, and received, the surrender of the blockhouse. Stough's men were paroled immediately and given a hand car to facilitate the removal of their wounded. After destroying the blockhouse and train, the Confederates moved off toward Romney.[106]

## 4 ANTIETAM FORD
Pickets from Cole's cavalry and the Fourteenth Pennsylvania Cavalry were driven from the ford; a combined force of Confederate infantry, artillery, and cavalry then crossed the river at Sheperdstown and Dam Number 4.[107]

## 5 HAGERSTOWN
Elements of the First West Virginia Cavalry skirmished with the enemy.

## WILLIAMSPORT
Companies B and H of the First West Virginia Cavalry skirmished with the enemy.[108]

## KEEDYSVILLE
By the end of August, General Hunter had returned from the lower end of the Shenandoah Valley where Early had bested him at Lynchburg the previous June. Making his headquarters in Frederick City, he commanded all Federal troops in that area. When reports reached Hunter that Early's army was again threatening to invade Maryland, he ordered Cole's cavalry to Hagerstown. Cole's battalion had recently been expanded to a full regiment, and was under

the temporary command of Lieutenant Colonel George W.F. Vernon.

Vernon learned from citizens of the area that the Confederates had established a picket post at Boonsboro. He moved the regiment to the summit of South Mountain, where it camped on the night of August 4. An advance guard under Captain Louis M. Zimmerman was stationed at the base of the mountain about three miles from Boonsboro. Scouts were sent out that night to learn the strength and location of the enemy. They reported a large force of Rebel cavalry five miles south of Boonsboro at Keedysville.

The next morning, the regiment moved out and engaged an enemy vedette on the Boonsboro Road. The Confederates exchanged a few shots and fell back, closely pursued by Captain Zimmerman and Company K. At the outskirts of Keedysville, the Union cavalry encountered a strong Southern picket line. Lieutenant Colonel Vernon heard the fresh outbreak of gunfire and brought up the regiment at a trot. He quickly realized that there were far more Rebels north of the river than he had been led to believe. Deploying his men left and right, Vernon ordered a charge that drove General A.J. Vaughn's brigade of Tennessee Cavalry back across Antietam Creek, where they were protected by a line of Confederate infantry. Vernon then broke off the engagement and retreated across South Mountain with all his wounded and a large number of prisoners. Union losses were heavy despite the success of the day. Company K alone, lost 18 of its 35 men during the engagement.[109]

# 7 MAJOR GENERAL PHILLIP H. SHERIDAN WAS GIVEN COMMAND OF THE MIDDLE MILITARY DIVISION

The total inability of the Union army to counter enemy activities in the lower Shenandoah Valley caused General Ulysses S. Grant to leave his headquarters at City Point, Virginia and come north to organize the final campaign against Early's army. Bypassing Washington, he went to Frederick County to meet General Hunter at the residence of Colonel C.K. Thomas on the Monocacy Battlefield on August 6.[110]

Grant was determined to consolidate the Middle Department and the Department of West Virginia, Washington and Susquehanna into a new organization known as the Middle Military Division.[111] General Hunter was relieved of his command. The next day, General Sheridan arrived by special train and was given command of the new division. Two divisions of cavalry were transferred to Sheridan from the Army of the Potomac and his orders were to follow the enemy, "to the death." [112]

## 22 COVE POINT

A sergeant and six men of the Fifth Massachusetts Colored Cavalry Regiment were sent to Cove Point to investigate a suspected blockade running operation. The detail stopped on the beach to eat breakfast and was fired on by an unseen enemy. The sergeant and two men were hit. The other four fled on foot, leaving their horses and equipment to be captured.[113]

# OCTOBER 1864

## 9 SANDY SPRINGS [RICKETT'S RUN]

Lieutenant Walter Bowie of Company F, Mosby's Rangers, and seven men crossed the Potomac River at Mathias Point and went to Port Tobacco where they captured 17 Federal soldiers and eight horses. After parolling the prisoners, Bowie led his men all the way to Annapolis in an abortive attempt to capture Governor Bradford.[114]

On the return trip, Bowie passed near Rockville and took the opportunity to rob the Sandy Springs store and collect a number of horses belonging to the normally peaceful Quakers in the area. Leaving the store after midnight, the raiders moved to within two or three miles of Rockville, where they camped for the remainder of the night.

As soon as the Rebels left the store, Al Thomas, a clerk and nephew of the owner, and his Uncle Gideon Gilpin, collected a possee of 17 men and set out to recapture their property. A trail of dropped plunder led them to a pine thicket along Rickett's Run. Hearing the citizens approaching, Bowie leaped on his horse and ordered his men to charge. William Ent, a local carriage maker, was standing behind a tree with a shotgun. When Bowie passed by he discharged a load of buckshot at the Rebel officer's head, knocking him to the ground.[115]

At this point, the possee "skedaddled." Bowie was taken to a nearby residence where he died a few hours later. His men recrossed the Potomac at Cheek's Ford.[116]

## 12-13 STATEWIDE VOTING ON NEW CONSTITUTION

Marylanders were given two days to vote on whether they wanted to accept or reject the new state constitution. Because of the magnitude of the issue and the strength of the Democratic Party in the state, special arrangements were made to allow some Maryland soldiers to cast their votes in the field. The results were as follows:

|  | FOR | AGAINST |
|---|---|---|
| HOME | 27,541 | 29,536 |
| SOLDIERS | 2,637 | 263 |
|  | 30,174 | 29,799 |

With a majority of only 375 votes, the new constitution was accepted. One can only imagine what the outcome would have been if the thousands of Marylanders in the Confederate Army had of been allowed to vote by proxy.[117]

## 14 RAID NEAR ADAMSTOWN

Captain William Chapman and about 80 men from Mosby's command crossed the Potomac River at White's Ford. Moving along the towpath, they burned eight or ten canal boats and their cargoes, while capturing a number of horses and mules. The telegraph line between Licksville and Adamstown was also cut.

Not finding any trains to attack on the Baltimore and Ohio line, the Confederates began to make the return trip to Virginia. Their rear guard was stalked by a company of Loudon County Rangers commanded by Captain Grubb. At one point, the Rebels turned on their pursuers, killing or capturing about a dozen and scattering the rest. When they reached the Chesapeake and Ohio Canal, they found a detachment of Union infantry tearing up the planks and throwing them in the water. Chapman ordered a charge, which dispersed the infantry. The floor of the bridge was soon re-laid and the raiding party returned to Virginia via Cheek's Ford.[118]

**18** GREAT WICOMICO BAY
The U.S. steam *Picket Boat No. 2* was enroute to Hampton Roads, Virginia from Baltimore when it developed engine trouble. Acting Ensign Andrew Stockholm put into the mouth of Reasons Creek for repairs. No sooner had the crew dropped anchor than the vessel was fired on from the shore line. Stockholm attempted to escape but ran aground. He then ordered the boat set afire and surrendered his crew.

# NOVEMBER 1864

**1** Slavery ceased to exist in the state of Maryland.[119]

**8** PRESIDENTIAL ELECTION OF 1864
Lincoln, with his new running mate, Andrew Johnson, defeated the Democratic nominees of General George B. McClellan and George H. Pendleton. Lincoln carried the state of Maryland, but not with an overwhelming majority. The results were as follows:[120]

|  | **LINCOLN** | **McCLELLAN** |
|---|---|---|
| HOME VOTE | 37,372 | 32,418 |
| SOLDIERS VOTE | 2,799 | 321 |
|  | 40,171 | 32,739 |

MARYLAND STATE ELECTION OF 1864
Thomas Swann was elected the third wartime Governor of Maryland.[121]

**9** FREEDMAN'S BUREAU ESTABLISHED
IN MARYLAND

Shortly after the Battle of Monocacy, General Lew Wallace was reinstated as Commander of the Middle Department. On November 9, he issued General Order Number 12, which established a Freedman's Bureau to aid the recently freed slaves in the state of Maryland. He placed Major William F. Este in charge of the new organization and instructed him to take over the Maryland Club House and use it to provide housing for the sick and homeless ex-slaves. The building was renamed "Freedman's Rest." [122]

# DECEMBER 1864

**6** Governor Bradford concluded his visit to the Army of the Potomac, during which time he presented each Maryland regiment with a new National and State flag. The flags were made of silk and were inscribed with the names of the battles each particular regiment had been engaged in.[123]

# CHAPTER SEVEN
# 1865

In 1865, the war took one final sweep across the state of Maryland. In the snow covered mountains of Western Maryland, Confederate raiders entered Cumberland and captured two Union generals without firing a shot. While this daring event excited the imagination of friend and foe alike, no one was actually hurt and the course of history was unchanged.

Unfortunately, this was not the case two months later when John Wilkes Booth fired what was perhaps the single most damaging shot of the war. The entire nation held its breath as the hunt for the president's assassin weaved its way through the swamps and creeks of Southern Maryland.

# JANUARY 1865

**4**    Maryland State Legislature convened in Annapolis.

**12** Thomas Swann was inaugurated as Governor of Maryland.[1] Swann was the third and last wartime governor of the state.

# FEBRUARY 1865

**17** ANNAPOLIS
Two steamers arrived bearing 1600 exchanged prisoners.[2] These men were cared for at the College Green Barracks on the campus of St. Johns College. This facility was also known as Division Number 2 of the Military General Hospital in Annapolis.

During the Civil War, Annapolis became the major receiving depot in the east for Union soldiers returning from Southern prisons. Exchanged or paroled, soldiers were given medical attention and new clothing at the College Green Barracks before being transferred to a larger facility known as Camp Parole a few miles outside of town.[3]

**18** CHARLESTON, SOUTH CAROLINA
Charleston, the "cradle of secession," was captured by General William T. Sherman's army.[4] South Carolina had been the first state to secede from the Union on December 20, 1860.[5]

**21** CUMBERLAND [THE CAPTURE OF GENERALS CROOK AND KELLY]
One of the last successful offensive military operations outside the Confederacy was planned by Private John B. Fay of McNeill's Partisan Rangers. Fay, a resident of Cumberland, along with a sixteen-year-old Missourian named Ritchie Hallar, crossed the Potomac River on the 19th. Their mission was to scout Union troop positions and to ascertain the exact location of Generals Crook and Kelly's sleeping quarters. The two men stopped at the home of an Irish secessionist named George Stanton, who gave them both information and shelter for the night. The next day, the scouts slipped back into Virginia. Fay sent Hallar to meet McNeill's command, leading them to their rendevous point near Romney, West Virginia.[6]

That night at the home of Vance Herriott, Fay gave Lieutenant

144

Jesse McNeill his report.[7] Cumberland was occupied by 6000 to 8000 Federal troops commanded by Brigadier General Hayes, Lightburn and Duval. The city was surrounded by an inner and outer ring of pickets, as well as irregular patrols. To the southeast lay Sheridan's army at Winchester. To the southwest were additional troops at New Creek. Getting into Cumberland would truly be only half of the battle.

Near sundown, McNeill gave the order to move out, and the Confederate column began to make its way through the snow covered mountains of West Virginia. With McNeill were 48 of his own men, nine from the Seventh Virginia, and six from the Eleventh Virginia Cavalry Regiments on loan from General Thomas Rosser's brigade. The raid was to be a local affair; most of the men with McNeill were from Cumberland. Sergeant James Daily's father was the proprietor of the Revere House where General Crook was making his headquarters; his sister was soon to be Mrs. Crook. Private Jacob Gassman's father owned the building. Jesse McNeill's family was also lately from Cumberland. Before his fathers death, they had talked of capturing General Kelly in retaliation for the rough treatment he had afforded Mrs. McNeill and the children.

After crossing the Potomac River, the raiders stopped at the home of Sam Brady to rest their horses and to secure the latest intelligence on enemy troop movements. Remounting, Lieutenant McNeill and Sergeant Vandiver set out as an advance guard. With them were Sergeant Joseph W. Kuykendall and Private Fay. The rest of the command, led by Lieutenant Isaac S. Welton, followed a safe distance behind. Two miles from Cumberland they captured a picket post manned by three men from Company D, Third Ohio Cavalry. After threatening to hang them, a German private revealed the counter sign "Ball's Gap." The prisoners were mounted on their horses and added to the column.

A mile from the city, a second picket post was discovered at the intersection of the Old Frostburg Turnpike. This was quickly surrounded and five men from the First West Virginia Infantry captured. Their weapons and ammunition were destroyed and the prisoners left behind, as they would only have been a hinderance to the fast moving column.

At this point, McNeill divided his command into squads, each with a particular mission. Sergeant Joseph Kuykendall, Company F,

Seventh Virginia Cavalry, and special scout to General Early, was given charge of the detail to capture Major General Benjamin F. Kelly. He had once been a prisoner of Kelly and knew what the man looked like. Sergeant George Vandiver with former hotel clerk Jacob Gassman, led the party that was to secure Major General George Crook. Fay and Hallar were ordered to destroy the telegraph.

The Confederates then proceeded down the road toward Cumberland. Turning onto Green Street, they skirted Courthouse Hill and crossed Wills Creek on the Chain Bridge. Riding up Baltimore Street, McNeill's men whistled Yankee tunes and joked with passing Union soldiers. At the Barnum House, one of the details stopped for General Kelly. Private Sprigg S. Lynn dismounted first and captured a sentry, whom he forced to lead Kuykendall's squad to Kelly's room.[8] Enroute, they captured Captain Thayer Melvin, Kelly's assistant adjutant general.[9] The two men were hustled outside and mounted double, with a Confederate soldier riding behind each, holding the reins.

At the Revere House, the capturing party found the front door locked. After knocking for sometime, a young colored boy named George Cooper finally opened the door. When asked if the general was in the hotel, he replied, "Yes, but don't tell him I tol you!" Room number 46 was entered by Gassman, Vandiver and Daily, who informed Crook he was a prisoner of war. When asked by whose authority, Vandiver told the general that he was General Rosser, and that Fitzhugh Lee's cavalry division had captured the city and its garrison. This took the fight out of Crook and he quickly dressed for the cold ride south.

Headquarters and other flags were taken as trophies of the occasion. Near the Chain Bridge, a number of horses were captured, including General Kelly's "Philippi." The column then headed out of town via Canal Street. A squad of 12 men was unexpectedly encountered along the canal and captured. Their arms were destroyed and the prisoners were left behind, as they would have slowed down the rate of travel.

Galloping towards Wiley's Ford, the Confederates were ordered to halt by a sentry on the canal bridge. The column did not halt and a sentry was heard to say, "Sergeant, shall I shoot?" A quick thinking Rebel replied, "If you do, I will place you under arrest. This is General Crook's bodyguard and we have no time to wait.

The Rebels are coming and we are going out to meet them." Thus fooling the guard, the raiders then sped toward safety of the Potomac.

McNeill's men had crossed the river and were several miles from Cumberland when the boom of a cannon sounded the alarm. All available Union cavalry were sent in pursuit of the Rebels, but failed to catch them. The next day, the two prisoners were delivered to General Early's headquarters.[10] McNeill's raid gave Southern spirits a brief lift, but a government clerk in Richmond looked upon the adventure in a more skeptic fashion when he wrote, "this is a little affair, but will make a great noise. We want 300,000 men in the field instead of 30."[11] Regardless of one's viewpoint, this was one of the most daring and successfully mounted operations of the war.

Two footnotes to this story are also worth telling. First, unknown to McNeill's men, Brigadier General Rutherford B. Hayes and Major William McKinley were also staying in the same hotels as the captured generals. Three generals, and two future presidents of the United States, would have indeed, made quite a catch.[12]

The second occurred the night after the raid. Miss Mary Clara Bruce, the future Mrs. Benjamin Kelly, was performing at a theater in Cumberland. When she sang, "He kissed me when he left," an irreverant, if not inaccurate, soldier yelled out, "No, I'll be damn if he did—McNeill didn't give him time." Thus ended the performance for the night.[13]

**25** EDWARDS FERRY
Lieutenant Chiswell led 22 men from Company B of E.V. White's Thirty-Fifth Virginia Battalion across the ice covered Potomac River at night. When they neared the north shore, they were fired on by two vedettes. The Confederates charged and overran the camp of the First Delaware Cavalry, wounding two men and capturing a third. Also captured were 14 horses and equipment, all of which was safely conveyed back to Virginia.[14]

# MARCH 1865

**4** Abraham Lincoln was inaugurated for his second term as President of the United States.[15]

**14** CHESAPEAKE BAY OFF INIGOES CREEK
After loading its cargo at the Port of St. Marys, the schooner *Champamero* set sail for the Chesapeake Bay. The *U.S.S. Wyandank* stopped the vessel off Inigoes Creek. When Acting Lieutenant Sylvanas Nicherson compared the actual cargo with the ships manifest, he found over half of it had not been recorded, including a large amount of gunpowder. The schooner was then seized for attempting to run the blockade.[16]

**18** The Confederate Congress in Richmond, Virginia adjourned for the last time.[17]

**31** CHESAPEAKE BAY OFF THE PATUXENT RIVER
Master John C. Braine, C.S.N., led a raiding party of 20 men out into the Chesapeake Bay in a yawl.[18] Their plan was to wait for an unsuspecting merchant vessel to come along. The disguised Confederates would then signal to indicate that they were sinking. When the vessel came along side they would board her.

On March 31, the 115-ton schooner *St. Mary's* left the port of St. Marys and fell into the trap. The Confederates seized her and put out for the open sea, where they captured the schooner *J.B. Spafford* bound for New York. The crew of the *St. Mary's* was transferred to the *J.B. Spafford* and the latter prize was released. Braine and his men then sailed to Nassau with cargo valued at $20,000.[19]

# APRIL 1865

**3** Richmond, Virginia was occupied by Federal troops.[20]

**5** CHESAPEAKE BAY
On April 5, the steamer *Harriet DeFord* was seized in the Chesapeake Bay about 20 miles below Annapolis. The boarding party, consisting of 27 men, was led by Captain Thaddeus Fitzhugh. As soon as the Federal authorities learned of this attack, a naval detach-

ment under the command of Lieutenant Commander Edward Hooker was sent to recover the steamer. Hooker found the *Harriet DeFord* in Dimer's Creek, Virginia, burned to the water line. Most of its cargo had been removed.[21]

**9** General Robert E. Lee surrendered the Army of Northern Virginia to General Ulysses S. Grant at Appomattox, Virginia.[22]

**12** Mobile, the last major city in the Confederacy, was surrendered.[23]

**14** General Robert Anderson returned the same flag to the staff at Fort Sumter that he had been forced to haul down on April 13, 1861.[24]

## 14-26 THE ASSASSINATION OF PRESIDENT LINCOLN

By mid-April, the Civil War ceased to be fought in the state of Maryland. Following the surrender of Lee's army, the commands of Mosby, McNeill, and White were disbanded. No longer would they fill the gaps between major Confederate invasions by splashing across the Potomac River to raid Union outposts, or to damage the Baltimore and Ohio Railroad. Despite this apparent end of hostilities, there was still one Confederate organization still intact and fully operational—the Secret Line.

From almost the beginning of the war, the Confederate government maintained a highly active underground operation in the Southern Maryland counties of Prince Georges, Charles and St. Marys. Working at night in small boats, these agents took recruits and mail pouches across the Potomac River. On the return trip, they brought back spies and top secret communications for Rebel agents operating as far north as Canada.[25] The points through which this traffic moved were known as "safe houses," of which, the home of Mary Surratt is the most famous.

149

It was within the framework of the Secret Line that John Wilkes Booth planned his attack on President Lincoln. There are many theories as to whether Booth's actions were authorized by the Richmond government, or simply an actor's attempt to gain eternal notoriety. The question may never be answered, and it is not within the scope of this text to address those issues.

Toward the end of 1864, an abduction plot was formalized by the Confederate Secret Service. The plan was to capture the president while he was taking one of his regular carriage drives in the neighborhood of the Washington Naval Yard. He would then be spirited away through Southern Maryland and conveyed across the Potomac by agents of the Secret Line.[26]

Booth, working with the Rebel agent John Surratt, often met at the boarding house owned by John's mother in Washington, D.C. He was also aware of the Surratt tavern in Surrattsville and other "safe houses" in Southern Maryland. Booth engaged the services of David Herold, George Atzerodt, Samuel Arnold, Edman Spangler, and Michael O'Laughlin in his abortive plans to capture Lincoln. Most of these men were Marylanders, and two had served in the Confederate Army.[27]

After the surrender of Lee's army and the fall of Richmond, Booth had nowhere to go even if he had succeeded in capturing Lincoln. Therefore, he converted the abduction plot into one of an assassination. It is quite conceivable that no one along the Secret Line knew of Lincoln's death until the day after the shooting.[28]

At about 10:30 on the night of April 14, Booth slipped into the rear of the Presidential box at Ford's Theater and fired a .44 caliber derringer at the back of Lincoln's head. The ball shattered the skull, lodging in the center of the president's brain. Major Henry Rathbone, a member of the presidential party that night, lunged at the assassin. Booth stabbed Rathbone with a hunting knife and hurdled over the balcony to the stage below. One of Booth's spurs caught in the flag adorning the presidential box, causing him to land off balance, breaking a bone in his left leg. Booth faced the startled audience and shouted, "Sic Semper Tyrannis," [thus always to tyrants] and he then limped as rapidly as possible across the stage. Booth bashed the conductor over the head when he tried to stop him, and made his way out the back door of the theater.[29]

The mortally wounded president was taken across the street to the home of William Peterson.[30] Surrounded by a number of army surgeons, government officials, and his wife, Lincoln died at 7:22 on the morning of April 15.[31]

Elsewhere in Washington, Lewis Paine unsuccessfully attempted to kill the Secretary of State William Henry Seward. He was later captured at the boarding house of Mrs. Surratt.[32]

Making his way through Washington, Booth met Herold at the Navy Yard Bridge. Crossing unchallenged, they rode toward Surrattsville. At the Surratt house, they stopped long enough to pick up two carbines and a supply of ammunition.

The two men then passed through the small hamlet of T.B. and did not stop until they reached the home of Doctor Samuel A. Mudd early the next day. Doctor Mudd set Booth's broken leg and Booth and Herold remained at the Mudd residence until the next night.[33] They then mounted their horses and rode off into Zachiah Swamp where they became lost for several hours. A black man, named Oswald Swan, happened to be passing through the area and he led the two strangers to the home of Samuel Cox, known as "Rich Hill."[34]

The three men arrived at "Rich Hill" about 4 a.m. on the 16th. Cox gave them food and hid them in the forest as it was too dangerous to let them stay in his home. He then sent his son to summon Thomas A. Jones.[35] Jones had been in charge of Confederate operations in Southern Maryland since the establishment of spy network in 1862. Despite the fact that the war was over, and Jones had every chance of going to the gallows with Booth if caught, he set about the task of getting the two men across the Potomac River. The entire area was inundated with cavalry patrols and government detectives. Booth was forced to lay out in the forest for six days while Jones watched for a chance to slip across the river.

On Friday, April 21, Jones learned that the cavalry patrols had moved to St. Marys county where Booth was rumored to be. Hurrying to the conspirator's hiding place that night, he reported, "the coast is clear and the darkness favors us. Let us make the attempt." Booth was mounted on Jones' horse and escorted by Herold. Jones preceeded the other two men by 60 yards as they made their way to his boat at Dent's Meadow.[36]

Several hours later, the trio reached the river's edge. Booth was loaded into the stern and given an oar to steer with. Herold took the bow. Jones gave them a compass bearing that would take them into Machodoc Creek on the Virginia shore. They were to seek aid from Mrs. Quesenberry who lived near the mouth of the creek. Their crossing was unsuccessful due to a strong tide that pushed the boat upriver. Herold returned to the Maryland shore later that night. The two men hid out throughout the day and succeeded in crossing the river the next night. Thus ended the last military operation in the state of Maryland during the Civil War.[37]

Booth and Herold were helped by the Southern sympathizers in Virginia as they made their way to the farm of Richard Garrett. Here on the night of April 26, a patrol of cavalry under the command of Lieutenant Edward Doughorty, Sixteenth New York Regiment, surrounded the barn in which the two men were hiding. Herold surrendered, but Booth chose to fight it out and was killed by Sergeant Boston Corbett.[38]

Following the death of Booth, Herold was taken to Washington where he was tried with the other conspirators. Scores of others were arrested including Jones, Cox, Dr. Mudd, and Mrs. Surratt. Following the trial of the century, Mary Surratt, David Herold, George Atzerodt, and Lewis Paine were executed on July 7, 1865.[39]

## 21  BALTIMORE

At 10:00 on the morning of April 21, 1865, the funeral train of Abraham Lincoln pulled into Camden Station. It had travelled from Washington on the Baltimore and Ohio line, passing through Annapolis Junction and Relay before making its first stop on the long and mournful journey to Springfield, ILL., where Lincoln was to be buried. Among the dignitaries accompanying the train to its final destination was John Garrett, President of the Baltimore and Ohio Railroad.[40]

When the train arrived, the coffin containing the martyred president was placed in a hearse with a rosewood frame and French plate glass windows three-quarters of an inch thick. A massive funeral procession, including politicians, generals, and soldiers from Fort McHenry, escorted the hearse through the jam-packed streets of Baltimore to the Merchants Exchange, where the coffin was opened for public viewing until 2:00 p.m. At that time it was returned to the waiting train for transportation to Harrisburg, Pennsylvania and another tightly scheduled public viewing.[41]

**26** General Joseph E. Johnson surrendered his army to General William T. Sherman at Durham, North Carolina.[42]

## THE ARREST OF BENJAMIN G. HARRIS

Benjamin Gwinn Harris was elected to the House of Representatives on November 4, 1863. His pro-slavery and anti-war views made him unpopular with his fellow congressmen, who at one time attempted to have him expelled from Congress. Harris was arrested at his home, Ellenborough, in St. Marys County on April 26, 1865, and charged with giving aid to the enemy. This occurred 17 days after Lee had surrendered at Appomattox.

Harris' arrest was the work of Major John M. Waite of the United States Army. Waite had detained two Confederate soldiers at Leonardtown, who were trying to make their way home to Baltimore. They were Sergeant Richard Chapman and Private William Read, recently of Company K, Thirty-Second Virginia Infantry. Waite ordered the two men to go to Ellenborough and request lodging for the night. Harris refused to take the soldiers in, but gave each one a dollar and told them to spend the night at the Leonardtown Hotel. This $2.00 donation landed the Congressman into the Old Capitol Prison in Washington, D.C.[43]

Despite the fact that the war was over and Harris was a civilian, he was tried by a military court and found guilty of violating the Articles of War. He was sentenced to three years imprisonment and disqualified from ever holding public office again. Such were the conditions of civil liberties in Maryland, even at the end of the Civil War. Fortunately for Harris, the conviction was overturned by President Johnson and he was able to return to his seat in Congress.[44]

# MAY 1865

**3** REDUCTION OF THE POTOMAC FLOTILLA

Secretary of the Navy, Giddeon Wells, ordered the Potomac Flotilla reduced to half strength due to the cessation of hostilities.[45]

# JUNE 1865

## 17 DEDICATION OF THE MONUMENT TO LADD AND WHITNEY

A monument to Privates Luther Crawford Ladd and Addison Otis Whitney was dedicated at Lowell, Massachusetts on June 17, 1865. Ladd and Whitney were killed in Baltimore on April 19, 1862 during the Pratt Street Riot.[46]

# CONCLUSION

On April 10, 1865, following the surrender at Appomattox, Virginia, General Robert E. Lee issued Special Order Number 9 which read in part, "After four years of arduous service, marked by unsurpassed courage and fortitude, the Army of Northern Virginia has been compelled to yield to overwhelming odds and resources..." What Lee wrote to his soldiers could have well been written for the entire country at that time. Each state, Union or Confederate, had endured "four years of arduous service," in the cause it felt right. Maryland, as did other border states, had contributed significantly to both sides in men, money, and personal suffering, which exemplified the real tragedy of the American Civil War.

# FOOTNOTES

CHAPTER ONE

[1] Oswald G. Villard, *John Brown A Biography Fifty Years After,* (Boston: 1910), pp. 402-403.

[2] Villard, pp. 406-407.

[3] Villard, p. 426.

[4] Villard, p. 429.

[5] Villard, p. 432.

Harold R. Manakee, *Maryland in the Civil War,* (Baltimore: 1961), p. 3.

[6] Villard, p. 433.

Edward Hungerford, *The Story of the Baltimore & Ohio Railroad 1807-1927,* (New York: 1928), pp. 340-342.

[7] Hungerford, p. 337.

[8] Villard, p. 434.

[9] Villard, p. 436.

[10] Villard, pp. 443-444.

[11] Manakee, p. 8.

[12] Manakee, pp. 8-10.

[13] Villard, p. 467.

## CHAPTER TWO

[1]Manakee, p. 14.

[2]Manakee, p. 16.

[3]Manakee, pp. 18-19.

[4]Emerson D. Fite, *The Presidential Campaign of 1860,* (New York: 1911), p. 107.

[5]Manakee, p. 14.

[6]Fite, p. 109.

[7]Manakee, p. 21.

[8]Robert B. Mosher, *Executive Register of the United States 1789-1902,* (Baltimore: 1903), p. 164.

## CHAPTER THREE

[1]*Between North and South,* Edited by Bayly E. Marks and Mark M. Schatz, (Cranberry, New Jersey: 1976), pp. 24-25.

[2]*Civil War Naval Chronology,* Naval History Division, Navy Department, (Washington, D.C.: 1971), Part VI, p. 12; hereafter referenced as *CWNC.*

[3]Ralph Newman and E. B. Long, *The Civil War Digest,* (New York: 1960), p. 7.

[4]William F. Mikay, *Campfire Sketches and Battlefield Echoes of 61-65,* (Springfield, Massachusetts: 1889), pp. 12-14.

[5]John W. Hanson, *Historical Sketch of the Old Sixth Regiment,* (Boston: 1866), p. 12.

[6]*Official Records,* (Washington, D.C.: Government Printing Office, 1887), Series I, Volume 2, p. 7; hereafter referenced as *OR's.*

[7]George W. Brown, *Baltimore and the 19th of April, 1861,* (Baltimore: 1887), pp. 46-53.

[8]Brown, pp. 56-57.

[9]Manakee, p. 38.

[10]Hon. J. Morrison Harris, "A Reminiscence of the Troublous Times of April 1861," *Maryland Historical Society Fund Publication,* No. 31, (Baltimore: 1891), pp. 21-25.

[11]Brown, pp. 60-64.

[12]Brown, p. 77.

[13]Benjamin F. Butler, *Butlers Book,* (Boston: 1892), pp. 194-95.

[14]Butler, pp. 201-202.

[15]*OR's,* Series I, Volume 2, p. 591.

[16]William J. Roehrembeck, *The Regiment that Saved the Capitol,* (New York: 1961), pp. 108-121.

[17] *CWNC,* Part I, p. 11.

[18] George E. Radcliffe, *Governor Thomas H. Hicks of Maryland and the Civil War,* (Baltimore: 1901), p. 63.

[19] Radcliffe, pp. 68-69.

[20] Radcliffe, pp. 71-72.

[21] Radcliffe, p. 74.

[22] Radcliffe, p. 95.

[23] *OR's,* Series I, Volume 2, p. 607.

[24] *CWNC,* Part VI, pp. 15-18.

[25] Butler, p. 223.

[26] *The Sun,* May 11, 1861.

[27] *The Raid of Ellicott Mills,* Published by the Howard County Historical Society, 1962, p. 32.

[28] Norman G. Ruckert, *Federal Hill,* (Baltimore: 1980), p. 18.

[29] *The Sun,* May 17, 1861.

[30] *The Sun,* May 20, 1861.

[31] *The Sun,* May 16, 1861.

[32] *The Sun,* May 18, 1861.

[33] *CWNC,* Part I, p. 14.

[34] *The Sun,* May 21, 1861.

[35] *CWNC,* Part I, p. 15.

[36] Walker Lewis, *Without Fear or Favor,* (Boston: 1965), pp. 450-452.

[37] Wills, pp. 25-29.

[38] *The Sun,* June 5, 1861.

[39] L.J. Loudermilk, *History of Cumberland,* pp. 397-398.

[40] *The Sun,* June 15, 1861.

[41] Frederick H. Dyer, *A Compendium of the War of the Rebellion,* (New York: 1959), Volume II, p. 759.

[42] *OR's,* Series I, Volume 2, pp. 109-110.
Otis F.R. Waite, *New Hampshire in the Great Rebellion,* (Claremont: 1870), pp. 72-73.

[43] *OR's,* Series I, Volume 2, pp. 111-112.
*The Union Army,* (Madison: 1908), Volume 5, p. 376.

[44] Loudermilk, pp. 400-401.

[45] *The Sun,* June 27, 1861.

[46] *OR's,* Series I, Volume 2, pp. 139-140.

[47] Mary Alice Wills, *The Confederate Blockade of Washington, D.C., 1861-1862,* (Parson, West Virginia: 1975), pp. 36-39.

[48]Manakee, pp. 62-63.

[49]Joseph Barry, *The Strange Story of Harpers Ferry,* (Sheperdstown: 1969), p. 106.

[50]*CWNC,* Part I, p. 18.

[51]*The Sun,* July 19, 1861.

[52]*OR's,* Series I, Volume 2, p. 123.

[53]*OR's Naval,* Volume 4, p. 566.

[54]Dyrer, Volume II, p. 759.

[55]*OR's,* Series I, Volume 5, p. 127.

[56]Warren H. Cudworth, *History of the First Regiment,* (Boston: 1866), pp. 86-94.

[57]*OR's,* Series I, Volume 5, pp. 193-197.

[58]*OR's,* Series I, Volume 5, pp. 197-199.

[59]*Military Operations of the Civil War,* Volume II of *Main Eastern Theater of Operations,* 2nd Fascicle, Section M, 1st Part, The National Archives, (Washington, D.C.: 1969), p. 86; hereafter referenced as *MO's.*

[60]*The Sun,* September 21, 1861.

[61]*Valley News Echo,* (Hagerstown, Volume 2, September 1961), No. 6.

[62]*OR's,* Series I, Volume 5, pp. 214-215.

[63]*OR's Naval,* Series I, Volume 4, p. 687.

[64]*OR's Naval,* Series I, Volume 4, p. 691.

[65]*The Sun,* September 25, 1861.

[66]*MO's,* p. 86.

[67]*The Sun,* October 3, 1861.

[68]*OR's,* Series I, Volume 5, p. 237.

[69]*MO's,* p. 85.

[70]*OR's,* Series I, Volume 5, p. 293.

[71]*OR's,* Series I, Volume 5, pp. 385-386.

[72]J. Thomas Scharf, *History of Maryland,* 1879, Volume III, p. 460.

[73]*Valley News Echo,* Volume 8, p. 2.

[74]Samuel P. Bates, *History of Pennsylvania Volunteers,* (Harrisburg: 1869), Volume I, p. 421.

[75]*CWNC,* Part I, pp. 34-37.

[76]*Chronicles of St. Mary's,* Volume 17, No. 2, February, 1969, pp. 263-265.

[77]Scharf, Volume III, p. 456.

[78] *OR's,* Series I, Volume 5, pp. 421-422.
[79] *Valley News Echo,* Volume 2, No. 8, p. 1.
[80] Scharf, Volume III, p. 460.
[81] *OR's,* Series I, Volume 5, p. 395.
[82] *The Sun,* December 11, 1861.
*The Sun,* December 12, 1861.
[83] *MO's,* p. 88.
[84] *OR's,* Series I, Volume 6, p. 469.
[85] *OR's,* Series I, Volume 5, p. 390.
[86] *The Sun,* December 21, 1861.
[87] *OR's,* Series I, Volume 5, p. 398.
[88] *OR's,* Series I, Volume 5, pp. 472-473.
[89] *The Sun,* December 20, 1861.
[90] C. Camper and J. Kirkley, *History of the First Regiment Maryland Volunteers,* (Washington: 1871), p. 209.

CHAPTER FOUR
[1] *CWNC,* Part II, p. 3.
[2] *OR's,* Series I, Volume 5, pp. 391-392.
[3] Scharf, Volume III, p. 466.
[4] *The Sun,* January 13, 1862.
[5] *The Sun,* January 29, 1861.
[6] Scharf, Volume III, p. 466.
[7] *The Democrat and News,* Cambridge, October 10, 1924.

[8] *The Delawarean,* Dover, March 15, 1962.
[9] John S. Spruance, *Delaware Stays in the Union,* (Newark: 1955), pp. 22-23.
[10] *The Democrat and News,* Cambridge, October 10, 1924.
[11] Wills, p. 147.
[12] *The Sun,* March 31, 1862.
[13] Festus P. Summers, *The Baltimore and Ohio in the Civil War,* (New York: 1939), pp. 115-116.
[14] Marks and Schatz, p. 309.
[15] Manakee, p. 57.
[16] *The Sun,* June 2, 1862.
[17] Scharf, Volume III, p. 491.
[18] *The Sun,* July 21, 1862.
[19] *The Sun,* July 29, 1862.

[20]Scharf, Volume III, p. 517.

[21]*OR's,* Series I, Volume 19, Part II, p. 590.

[22]*MO's,* p. 89.

[23]*OR's,* Series I, Volume 19, Part I, p. 1019.

[24]*MO's,* p. 95.

[25]R.L.T. Beale, *History of the Ninth Virginia Cavalry,* (Richmond: 1899), p. 37.

[26]*Southern Historical Society Papers,* (Millwood, New York: 1977), Volume III, p. 284, hereafter referenced as *SHSP.*

[27]*The Union Army,* (Madison, Wisconsin: 1908), Volume 6, p. 700.

[28]*The Union Army,* Part I, pp. 208, 815, 825.

[29]*The Union Army,* Part I, p. 545.

[30]*36th Annual Report of the Baltimore and Ohio Railroad,* pp. 55-56.

[31]*OR's,* Series I, Volume 19, Part I, p. 208.

[32]*Medical and Surgical History of the War of the Rebellion,* (Washington, D.C.: Government Printing Office, 1876), Part II, Volume I, p. LVII, hereafter referenced as *MASH.*

[33]Henry Kyd Douglas, *I Rode with Stonewall,* (New York: 1940), pp. 152-153.

[34]Beale, pp. 37-38.

*OR's,* Series I, Volume 19, Part I, p. 209.

[35]*Valley News Echo,* Volume III, p. 3.

[36]*OR's,* Series I, Volume 19, Part I, p. 416.

[37]*SHSP,* Volume 13, pp. 417-419.

[38]*SHSP,* Volume 13, pp. 209, 823.

[39]James V. Martin, *The Gleam of Bayonets,* (New York: 1965), p. 133.

[40]*OR's,* Series I, Volume 19, Part I, pp. 852-853.

[41]*OR's,* Series I, Volume 19, Part I, pp. 541-544.

[42]*OR's,* Series I, Volume 19, Part I, p. 546.

[43]*OR's,* Series I, Volume 19, Part I, p. 854.

[44]*OR's,* Series I, Volume 19, Part I, p. 528.

[45]*OR's,* Series I, Volume 19, Part I, p. 449.

[46]*OR's,* Series I, Volume 19, Part I, pp. 823-825.

[47]D.C. Freeman, *Lee's Lieutenants,* (New York: 1943), Volume II, pp. 172-173.

[48]*OR's,* Series I, Volume 19, Part I, pp. 818-819.

[49]*OR's,* Series I, Volume 19, Part I, p. 417.

[50]John W. Schildt, *September Echoes,* (Middletown: 1960), p. 33.

[51]*Battles and Leaders of the Civil War*, Volume II, pp. 566-567; hereafter referenced as *B&L*.

[52]Martin, p. 177.

[53]*OR's*, Series I, Volume 19, Part I, p. 818.

[54]*OR's*, Series I, Volume 19, Part I, p. 375.

[55]*OR's*, Series I, Volume 19, Part I, pp. 826-829.

[56]*OR's*, Series I, Volume 19, Part I, pp. 375-376.

[57]*OR's*, Series I, Volume 19, Part I, p. 861.

[58]*OR's*, Series I, Volume 19, Part I, p. 827.

[59]Freeman, Volume II, p. 199.

[60]Beale, pp. 39-40.

[61]*OR's*, Series I, Volume 19, Part I, p. 204.

[62]*CWNC*, Part II, p. 97.

[63]*The Union Army*, Volume 5, p. 34.

[64]*The Union Army*, Volume 6, p. 783.

[65]*The Union Army*, Volume 5, p. 33.

[66]Freeman, Volume II, pp. 221-225.

[67]Frederic Tilberg, *Antietam*, (Washington, D.C.: 1960), p. 47.

[68]*OR's*, Series I, Volume 19, Part I, pp. 831-832.

[69]*OR's*, Series I, Volume 19, Part I, p. 212.

[70]*OR's*, Series I, Volume 19, Part I, p. 340.

[71]*OR's*, Series I, Volume 19, Part I, p. 346.

[72]*The Union Army*, Volume 5, p. 132.

[73]Dyer, Volume II, p. 761.

[74]Harry R. Newman, *Maryland and the Confederacy*, (Annapolis: 1976), pp. 139-140.

[75]John W. Schildt, *Four Days in October*, 1982, p. 9.

[76]*OR's*, Series I, Volume 19, Part II, p. 57.

[77]*OR's*, Series I, Volume 19, Part II, p. 33.

[78]*OR's*, Series I, Volume 19, Part II, pp. 37-38.

[79]*OR's*, Series I, Volume 19, Part II, p. 39.

[80]*OR's*, Series I, Volume 19, Part II, p. 48.

[81]*OR's*, Series I, Volume 19, Part II, p. 39.

[82]*The Sun*, October 17, 1862.

[83]*The Sun*, October 24, 1862.

[84]*CWNC*, Part II, p. 107.

[85]*CWNC*, Part II, p. 108.

[86]*CWNC*, Part II, p. 108.

[87]Ezra J. Warner, *Generals in Blue*, (Ann Arbor: 1972), p. 57.

[88]*CWNC,* Part II, p. 110.

[89]*The Sun,* November 29, 1862.

[90]Scharf, p. 523.

[91]F.W. Myers, *The Comanches, A History of White's Battalion Virginia Cavalry,* (Marietta: 1956), pp. 146-148.

CHAPTER FIVE

[1]Newman and Long, p. 26.

[2]Newman and Long, p. 27.

[3]Regina C. Hammett, *History of St. Mary's County, Maryland,* (Ridge, Maryland: 1977), p. 112.

[4]*The Union Army,* Volume 5, p. 28.

[5]*37th Annual Report of the Baltimore and Ohio Railroad,* pp. 45-56.

[6]*37th Annual Report of the Baltimore and Ohio Railroad,* pp. 45-46.

[7]W.N. McDonald, *A History of the Laurel Brigade,* (Baltimore: 1907), p 124.

[8]*The Glade Star,* Volume 3, No. 5, p. 71.

[9]James J. Williamson, *Mosby's Rangers,* (New York: 1896), pp. 69-71.

[10]*OR's,* Series I, Volume 27, Part II, p. 549.

[11]*OR's,* Series I, Volume 27, Part II, pp. 193-194.

[12]Meyers, pp. 188-191.

[13]*37th Annual Report of the Baltimore and Ohio Railroad,* p. 49.

[14]Loudermilk, pp. 409-412.

[15]J.W. Schildt, *Roads to Gettysburg,* (Parsons: 1978), p. 158.

[16]C.A. Newcomer, *Cole's Cavalry,* (Freeport: 1895), p. 51.

[17]*37th Annual Report of the Baltimore and Ohio Railroad,* p. 49.

[18]Newcomer, p. 51.

[19]Beale, pp. 79-80.

[20]Freeman, pp. 64-65.

[21]*37th Annual Report of the Baltimore and Ohio Railroad,* p. 49.

[22]*OR's,* Series I, Volume 27, Part II, p. 694.

[23]*Just South of Gettysburg,* F.S. Klein, Editor, (Lancaster: 1974), pp. 44-48.

[24]*OR's,* Series I, Volume 27, Part II, pp. 201-203.

[25]*OR's,* Series I, Volume 27, Part II, p. 695.

[26]Col. James Wallace, *Our March to Gettysburg,* Printed in *Our*

*Country,* Edited by Mrs. Lincoln Phelps, (Baltimore: 1864), pp. 60-61.

[27]*SHSP,* Volume 2, p. 66.

[28]*OR's,* Series I, Volume 27, Part I, p. 193.

[29]*OR's,* Series I, Volume 27, Part II, p. 760.

[30]*OR's,* Series I, Volume 27, Part I, p. 994.

[31]*OR's,* Series I, Volume 27, Part I, pp. 1035-1036.

[32]*OR's,* Series I, Volume 27, Part I, p. 1009.

[33]*OR's,* Series I, Volume 27, Part I, p. 1014.

[34]Beale, p. 92.

[35]*OR's,* Series I, Volume 27, Part I, p. 1006-1007.

[36]Beale, p. 93.

[37]*OR's,* Series I, Volume 27, Part II, p. 702.

[38]*OR's,* Series I, Volume 27, Part I, p. 1110.

[39]Beale, p. 94.

[40]*OR's,* Series I, Volume 27, Part I, p. 1006.

[41]*OR's,* Series I, Volume 27, Part I, p. 995.

[42]*OR's,* Series I, Volume 27, Part I, pp. 1014-1015.

[43]*B&L,* Volume 3, Part II, p. 424.

[44]Schildt, p. 89.

[45]*B&L,* Volume 3, Part II, pp. 426-427.

[46]*OR's,* Series I, Volume 27, Part II, p. 438.

[47]*B&L,* p. 427.

[48]*OR's,* Series I, Volume 27, Part I, p. 928.

[49]*OR's,* Series I, Volume 27, Part I, p. 935.

[50]*OR's,* Series I, Volume 27, Part II, pp. 437-438.

[51]*OR's,* Series I, Volume 27, Part II, p. 499.

[52]*B&L,* pp. 427-428.

[53]*OR's,* Series I, Volume 27, Part I, p. 193.

[54]*B&L,* p. 428.

[55]*SHSP,* Volume II, pp. 69-70.

[56]*OR's,* Series I, Volume 27, Part I, p. 193.

[57]*OR's,* Series I, Volume 27, Part I, pp. 948-949.

[58]*OR's,* Series I, Volume 27, Part II, p. 754.

[59]*OR's,* Series I, Volume 27, Part II, p. 949.

[60]*MASH,* p. 6.

[61]*OR's,* Series I, Volume 27, Part II, pp. 760-761.

[62]Camper and Kirkley, pp. 101-105.

[63]*OR's,* Series I, Volume 27, Part II, p. 704.

[64]*OR's,* Series I, Volume 27, Part III, pp. 602-603.

[65]*OR's,* Series I, Volume 27, Part II, p. 704.

[66]*OR's,* Series I, Volume 27, Part III, p. 603.

[67]*OR's,* Series I, Volume 27, Part II, p. 704.

[68]*OR's,* Series I, Volume 27, Part II, p. 280.

[69]*OR's,* Series I, Volume 27, Part I, p. 193.

[70]*OR's,* Series I, Volume 27, Part I, p. 941.

[71]*OR's,* Series I, Volume 27, Part II, pp. 274-275.

[72]*OR's,* Series I, Volume 27, Part I, p. 222.

[73]Jacob Stonebreaker, *A Rebel of 61,* pp. 53-54.

[74]*OR's,* Series I, Volume 27, Part I, p. 936.

[75]Stonebreaker, p. 54.

[76]*OR's,* Series I, Volume 27, Part I, p. 296.

[77]*OR's,* Series I, Volume 27, Part I, p. 667.

[78]*OR's,* Series I, Volume 27, Part I, p. 455.

[79]*OR's,* Series I, Volume 27, Part II, pp. 704-705.

[80]*OR's,* Series I, Volume 27, Part II, p. 765.

[81]John O. Casler, *Four Years in the Stonewall Brigade,* (Dayton: 1971), p. 179.

[82]*OR's,* Series I, Volume 27, Part I, p. 999.

[83]*OR's,* Series I, Volume 27, Part I, p. 991.

[84]*OR's,* Series I, Volume 27, Part II, p. 648.

[85]*OR's,* Series I, Volume 27, Part I, p. 990.

[86]*OR's,* Series I, Volume 27, Part II, p. 648.

[87]*OR's,* Series I, Volume 27, Part I, p. 990.

[88]*OR's,* Series I, Volume 27, Part II, p. 648.

[89]*OR's,* Series I, Volume 27, Part II, p. 672.

[90]*OR's,* Series I, Volume 27, Part II, p. 667.

[91]Casler, p. 178.

[92]Manakee, p. 89.

[93]Manakee, p. 92.

[94]Francis T. Miller, *Photograph History of the Civil War*, (New York: 1912), Volume 7, p. 90.

[95]*CWNC,* Part III, p. 129.

[96]Myers, p. 217.

[97]*Chronicles of St. Mary's,* Volume 27, p. 64.

[98]*The Sun,* September 15, 1863.

[99]*CWNC,* Part III, pp. 140-141.

[100]*The Sun,* September 25, 1863.

[101] *The Sun,* November 4, 1863.
[102] *CWNC,* Part III, p. 157.


CHAPTER SIX

[1] J. Thomas Scharf, *History of Maryland,* Hatboro Pa. Edition 1967, Volume III, p. 574.
[2] *CWNC,* Part IV, p. 15.
[3] Scharf, Volume III, p. 603.
[4] Scharf, p. 577.
[5] Scharf, p. 582.
[6] *OR's,* Series I, Volume 37, Part I, pp. 71-72.
[7] *OR's Naval,* Series I, Volume 5, p. 433.
[8] *CWNC,* Part IV, p. 61.
[9] *The Frederic Examiner,* May 25, 1864.
[10] *CWNC,* Part IV, p. 70.
[11] Scharf, p. 602.
[12] Dyer, Volume II, p. 763.
[13] *38th Annual Report of the Baltimore and Ohio Railroad,* p. 57.
[14] *OR's,* Series I, Volume 37, Part I, pp. 185-186.
[15] *OR's,* Series I, Volume 37, Part I, p. 219.
[16] Dyer, Volume II, p. 763.
[17] Williams, p. 184.
[18] *OR's,* Series I, Volume 37, Part I, p. 219.
[19] *OR's,* Series I, Volume 37, Part II, p. 76.
[20] Richard R. Duncan, "Maryland's Reaction to Early's Raid," *Maryland Historical Magazine,* Volume 64, Number 3, Fall 1969, p. 250.
[21] *OR's,* Series I, Volume 37, Part I, p. 337.
[22] Duncan, pp. 251-252.
[23] *MO's,* Volume II, p. 85.
[24] Newcomer, p. 129.
[25] *MO's,* Volume II, p. 86.
[26] *OR's,* Series I, Volume 37, Part I, p. 219.
[27] *OR's,* Series I, Volume 37, Part I, p. 194.
[28] *OR's,* Series I, Volume 37, Part I, p. 219.
[29] *OR's,* Series I, Volume 37, Part I, p. 194.
[30] Dyer, Volume II, p. 763.
[31] *OR's,* Series I, Volume 37, Part II, p. 110.

[32]*OR's,* Series I, Volume 37, Part I, p. 179.

[33]*OR's,* Series I, Volume 37, Part I, p. 194.

[34]Glenn H. Worthington, *Fighting for Time,* (Baltimore: 1932), pp. 81-84.

[35]*OR's,* Series I, Volume 37, Part I, pp. 195.

[36]*OR's,* Series I, Volume 37, Part I, p. 220.

[37]Worthington, p. 105.

[38]*OR's,* Series I, Volume 37, Part I, pp. 193-196.

[39]Worthington, p. 107.

[40]Worthington, pp. 118-119.

[41]Worthington, pp. 123-126.

[42]Worthington, p. 111.

[43]Worthington, pp. 113-116.

[44]*OR's,* Series I, Volume 37, Part I, pp. 351-352.

[45]Frank Vandiver, *Jubal's Raid,* (New York: 1960), pp. 118-119.

[46]*OR's,* Series I, Volume 37, Part I, p. 197.

[47]*OR's,* Series I, Volume 37, Part I, pp. 199-200.

[48]*OR's,* Series I, Volume 37, Part I, p. 348.

[49]*OR's,* Series I, Volume 37, Part I, p. 352.

[50]*OR's,* Series I, Volume 37, Part I, pp. 220-221.

[51]*MO's,* p. 90.

[52]*OR's,* Series I, Volume 37, Part I, p. 204.

[53]*OR's,* Series I, Volume 37, Part I, pp. 248-249.

[54]*OR's,* Series I, Volume 37, Part I, p. 170.

[55]Williams, p. 189.

[56]*OR's,* Series I, Volume 27, Part I, pp. 254-257.

[57]Worthington, pp. 182-183.

[58]Worthington, pp. 176-178.

[59]*OR's,* Series I, Volume 27, Part I, p. 348.

[60]*OR's,* Series I, Volume 27, Part I, p. 236.

[61]*OR's,* Series I, Volume 27, Part I, p. 275.

[62]Vandiver, p. 156.

[63]*OR's,* Series I, Volume 27, Part I, p. 276.

[64]John H. Cramer, *Lincoln Under Enemy Fire,* (Baton Rouge: 1948), pp. 20-22.

[65]*OR's,* Series I, Volume 27, Part I, pp. 276-277.

[66]Douglas, pp. 295-296.

[67]W.W. Goldsboro, *The Maryland Line in the Confederate Army 1861-1865,* (New York: 1972), p. 204.

[68]*SHSP,* Volume 30, p. 218.

[69]*Confederate Veterans Magazine,* Volume 20, No. 2, Nashville, 1912, pp. 69-70.

[70]*Maryland Historical Magazine,* "Maryland's Reaction to Early's Raid in 1864," Fall 1969, Volume 64, No. 3, p. 265.

[71]Harry Gilmor, *Four Years in the Saddle,* (New York: 1866), p. 190.

[72]*SHSP,* pp. 218-219.

[73]George W. Booth, *Personal Reminiscences of a Maryland Soldier in the War Between the States 1861-1865,* (Baltimore: 1898), p. 124.

[74]Booth, p. 124.

[75]*Maryland Historical Magazine,* Volume 64, No. 3, p. 220.

[76]Booth, p. 124.

[77]*38th Annual Report of the Baltimore and Ohio Railroad,* p. 62.

[78]Henry C. Mettam, "Civil War Memories, 1st Maryland Cavalry, CSA" (Ed. Samuel H. Miller), *Maryland Historical Magazine* (June 1963), Volume 58, pp. 157-158.

[79]Booth, pp. 124-125.

[80]Gilmor, pp. 192-195.

[81]*OR's,* Series I, Volume 37, Part I, pp. 225-226.

[82]*OR's,* Series I, Volume 37, Part I, p. 230.

[83]Gilmor, p. 196.

[84]*OR's,* Series I, Volume 37, Part I, p. 230.

[85]Gilmor, pp. 197-203.

[86]*SHSP,* Volume 30, pp. 222-223.

[87]*MASH,* Part II, Volume I, p. 213.

[88]*CWNC,* Part IV, p. 89.

[89]Worthington, pp. 202-203.

[90]*SHSP,* Volume 30, p. 223.

[91]*OR's,* Series I, Volume 37, Part I, p. 286.

[92]*OR's,* Series I, Volume 37, Part II, p. 472.

[93]*OR's,* Series I, Volume 37, Part I, p. 354.

[94]*OR's,* Series I, Volume 37, Part I, pp. 342-343.

[95]Newcomer, pp. 142-143.

[96]*OR's,* Series I, Volume 37, Part I, p. 343.

[97]*OR's,* Series I, Volume 37, Part II, p. 529.

[98]Williams, p. 197.

[99] *OR's,* Series I, Volume 37, Part I, p. 355.

[100] *OR's,* Series I, Volume 37, Part I, p. 188.

[101] *MASH,* Part I, p. 329.

[102] *OR's,* Series I, Volume 37, Part I, p. 188.

[103] *OR's,* Series I, Volume 37, Part I, pp. 355-356.

[104] *OR's,* Series I, Volume 37, Part I, p. 189.

[105] Booth, p. 132.

[106] *OR's,* Series I, Volume 37, Part I, p. 189.

[107] *The Union Army,* Volume 5, p. 37.
MO's, p. 92.

[108] Dyer, Volume II, p. 764.

[109] Newcomer, pp. 144-151.

[110] Worthington, pp. 205-206.

[111] U.S. Grant, *Personal Memoirs,* (New York: 1885), Volume II, p. 582.

[112] Grant, p. 318.

[113] *The Union Army,* Volume V, p. 324.

[114] Williams, p. 256.

[115] Harold B. Stabler, *Some Recollections, Anecdotes, and Tales of Old Times,* 1962, pp. 19-22.

[116] Williams, p. 165.

[117] Scharf, Volume III, p. 597.

[118] Williams, p. 264.

[119] *The Frederic Examiner,* November 2, 1864.

[120] Scharf, Volume III, p. 642.

[121] Marks and Schatz, p. 396.

[122] Scharf, Volume III, pp. 598-599.

[123] *The Frederic Examiner,* December 14, 1864.

## CHAPTER SEVEN

[1] *The Sun,* January 12, 1865.

[2] *The Sun,* February 18, 1865.

[3] Tench F. Tilghman, "The College Green Barracks: St. Johns During the Civil War," *Maryland Historical Magazine* Volume XLV, June 1950, No. 2, p. 8485.

[4] Newman and Long, p. 50.

[5] V.A. Swanberg, *First Blood: The Story of Fort Sumter,* (New York: 1957), p. 79.

[6]McDonald, pp. 343-344.

[7]Virgil C. Jones, *Gray Ghosts and Rebel Raiders*, (New York: 1956), p. 357.

[8]McDonald, pp. 343-349.

[9]*OR's,* Series I, Volume 46, Part II, p. 621.

[10]McDonald, pp. 349-351.

[11]John B. Jones, *A Rebel War Clerks Diary,* Edited by Earl C. Miers, (New York: 1958), p. 507.

[12]J.W. Duffey, *Two Generals Kidnapped and A Race For the Prize,* (Washington, D.C.: 1927), p. 12.

[13]Duffey, p. 14.

[14]Myers, p. 357.

[15]Newman and Long, p. 50.

[16]*CWNC,* Part V, p. 61.

[17]Newman and Long, p. 50.

[18]*OR's Naval,* Series I, Volume 5, pp. 540-541.

[19]*CWNC,* Part V, p. 73.

[20]Newman and Long, p. 51.

[21]*CWNC,* Part V, p. 80.

[22]Newman and Long, p. 51.

[23]Newman and Long, p. 51.

[24]D.M. Kunhardt and P.B. Kunhardt, Jr., *Twenty Days,* (New York: 1965), p. 20.

[25]Thomas A. Jones, *John Wilkes Booth,* (Chicago: 1893), p. 13.

[26]Jones, pp. 39-40.

[27]*Civil War Times Illustrated*, Volume III, Number 4, (Harrisburg: 1965), p. 7, hereafater referenced as *CWTI.*

[28]Jones, pp. 43-46.

[29]*CWTI,* Volume III, Number 4, p. 16.

[30]Kunhardt and Kunhardt, p. 46.

[31]Kunhardt and Kunhardt, pp. 78-80.

[32]Guy W. Moore, *The Case of Mrs. Surratt,* (Norman: 1954), pp. 16-19.

[33]Jones, pp. 49-55.

[34]Jones, p. 62.

[35]Jones, pp. 71-73.

[36]Jones, pp. 98-101.

[37]Jones, pp. 109-111.

[38]Kunhardt and Kunhardt, p. 176.

[39]Kunhardt and Kunhardt, pp. 204-205.

[40]*The Sun,* April 21, 1865.
[41]Kunhardt and Kunhardt, p. 141.
[42]Newman and Long, p. 51.
[43]Hammett, p. 117.
[44]Marks and Schatz, p. 359.
[45]*CWNC,* Part V, p. 97.

# INDEX

Abbott, 54
Accomac County, Va., 34
Adamstown, 133, 140
Ady's Hotel, 129
Alexander, F.W., 104, 105
*Alexandria,* 93
Alexandria, Va., 20-21
*Alliance,* 93
Altamont, 72
*Anacostia, U.S.S.,* 22, 23
Antietam, 42, 62, 68
Antietam Bridge, 105
Antietam Creek, 103
Antietam Ford, 29, 137
Anderson, Jeremiah, 2
Anderson, Robert, 10, 149
*Ann Hamilton,* 98
Annapolis, 13, 15-18, 32, 98, 99, 130, 143, 144
Annapolis, Department of, 16
Annapolis and Elkridge RR, 13, 14
Annapolis Junction, 14, 15, 152
Aquia Creek, Va., 43
*Arctic,* 62
Army of Northern Virginia, 52, 55, 63, 73, 79, 88, 107, 149
Army of the Potomac, 46, 50, 65, 68, 72, 77, 85, 135, 139, 142
Army of the Shenandoah, 134
Arnold, Samuel, 150
Ashby, Turner, 37
Atkins, William A., 42, 132
Atzerodt, George, 150, 152

Averell, William W., 134
Aylett, William A., 83
Babcock, William L., 68
Bailey, Capt., 128
Balls Bluff, Va., 32
Baltimore City, 6, 9-13, 18-21, 25, 43, 98, 100, 105, 107, 125, 152
Baltimore City Police Department, 11, 12, 20, 25, 69
Baltimore County, 126
Baltimore and Ohio RR, 2, 3, 6, 14, 17, 20, 23, 24, 43, 44, 47, 48, 65, 73, 105, 107, 126, 152
*Baltimore Exchange,* 29, 69
*Baltimore Republican,* 92
Banks, Nathaniel, 29
Barnesville, 47, 49, 60
Barnett's Battalion, 82
Barnum House, 146
Barr, Capt., 29
Barton, W. Mitchell, 52
Bath, WV., 40
Baylor, W.S.H., 40
Beale, R.L.T., 62
Beall, John F., 93
Bear Valley, 87
Beauregard, P.G.T., 10
Beaver Creek, 87
Beaver Creek Bridge, 86
Becker, Anton, 27
Bedford, Pa., 24
Bell, John, 6, 7
Beltsville, 126, 131
Berlin, 30, 31, 33, 46, 47

Besley, Horace, 24
Biddle, Nickoles, 11, 58
Biggs, J.W., 48
Bird, P.H., 48
Bishop, John L., 44
Black, John L., 83
Blackfords Ford, 63
Blackistone, Henry, 125
Blackistone Island, 99
Bladensburg, 16, 28
Blair, Montgomery, 121
Blake, George S., 13
Blakely, William, 119
Bloody Lane, 63
Bolivar Heights, WV, 41, 86, 101
Bolton Station, 10
Bolza, Charles E., 91
Bonifant, Washington, 20
Boonsboro, 49, 55, 62, 86, 138
Booth, George W., 127
Booth, John W., 116, 150-152
Bowie, Walter, 139
Bowman, 78
Boyd's Hole, Va., 41
Dr. Brace, wife of, 23
Bradford, Augustus W., 33, 35, 41, 45, 94, 112, 125, 139, 142
Brady, Sam, 145
Braine, John C., 148
Braine, Lt. Com., 130
Brawner, Capt., 74
Breckinridge, John, 7, 123
Brien, Lt., 50
Briscoe, Alexander, M., 132, 133
Bristol, 28
Brockenbrough, J.M., 25
Brown, A.L., 105, 108

Brown, George W., 12, 13, 29, 58, 69
Brown, John, 1, 2, 56
Brown, John, Jr., 2
Brown, Owen, 2
Brownsville, 103
Brownsville Gap, 52, 55
Buchanan, James, 3
Buckley, F.A., 75
Burkittsville, 54
Burks, R.S., 48
Burnside, Ambrose E., 50, 68
Burnside Bridge, 63, 68, 72
Bush River, 12
Butler, Benjamin F., 13, 15-18, 110
Butler, M.C., 65
Cadwalader, George, 21
Calvert County, 28, 32
Camden Station, 11, 152
Cameron, Simon, 29
Camp Butler, 18
Camp Parole, 117, 144
Camp Union, 28
Capitola, 67
Carbury House, 122
Carlisle, Pa., 102
Carlisle Barracks, 132
Carlton, Capt., 53
Carmichael, Richard B., 44, 112
Carroll Guards, 32
Carroll, John L., 126
Carroll, John N., 125
Carson, James H., 37
Cary, Hettie, 14
Cary, Jennie, 14
Catlin, Lynde, 106
Catoctin Creek, 51, 74, 75
Catoctin Mountain, 51, 104

Chambersburg, Pa., 2, 66, 135
Chamblis, John R., 80
*Champamero,* 148
Chapin, Lt., 48
Chaplin, J.C., 25
Chaplin, R.H., 47
Chapman, Richard, 153
Chapman, William, 140, 141
Charles County, 149
Charlotte Hall, 32
Cheek's Ford, 133, 140, 141
Cherry Run, 132
Chesapeake Bay, 67, 91, 93, 98
Chew's Battery, 48, 55, 86, 88
Chiswell, George W., 68
Claflin, Ira W., 84
Clark, D.W.C., 78
Clear Springs, 87, 132
Clemen's House, 38
Clendenin, D.R., 103, 104, 118, 119
Cobb, Howell, 61
Cobb's Legion, 54
Cockeysville, 12, 21, 125, 127
Cockpit Point, 35, 43
*Coeur DeLion,* U.S.S., 93, 100
Cole, William G., 106
College Green Barracks, 144
Colonization Society of Maryland, 6
Colston, R.T., 37
Confederate Signal Corps, 50
Confederate Secret Service, 150
Conowingo Bridge, 128
Conrads Ferry, 23, 28, 30, 32, 48, 120
*Constitution, U.S.S.,* 13
Constitutional Unionists Party, 6, 15

Cooksville, 77
Cooper, George, 146
Corbit, Boston, 152
Corbit, Charles, 78
Corliss, Augustus W., 53
Courtney's Battery, 83
Cove Point, 139
Cox, Samuel, 151, 152
Craddock, Mr., 129
Crampton's Gap, 54, 55, 60, 61
Cranberry Summit, 73
Crook, George, 131, 144-146
Crown, J.R., 74
Crum's Ford, 108
*Crusader, U.S.S.,* 99
Cumberland 23, 24, 44, 75, 134, 135, 137, 144, 145
Cumberland Continentals, 24
Dahlgren, John A., 20
Daily, James, 145, 146
Dam #4, 36, 132, 137
Dam #5, 35, 36
*Dana, U.S.S.,* 27
Davis, George E., 109
Davis, Jefferson, 45, 47, 124
Davis, J.L., 80
Davis, T. Sturgis, 76, 103
Day, Ishmael, 127
Dekorponay, Gabriel, 37
Delaney, Lt., 133
Delaware, 42, 43, 127
Delaware Military Units, 1st Cav., 77; 7th Inf., 128
Delmar, 42
Democratic Party, 6, 7, 140
Dent's Meadow, 151
Devin, Thomas C., 87
Dickinson, Charles, 18
Dimer's Creek, Va., 149

District of Columbia Military
Units, 2nd Bat. Inf., 23; 8th
Bat. Inf., 27; Militia, 120
Dix, John A., 34, 43, 44, 112
Dodd, Thomas, 84
Donaldsonville Battery, 82
Dorsey, N.W., 75
Doubleday, Abner, 25
Doughorty, Edward, 152
Douhoregan Manor, 126
Douglas, Henry K., 49, 123
Douglas, Stephen A., 6, 7
Dover, De., 42
Downs, J.S., 72
Downsville, 84
Draper, Lt., 102
Dunker Church, 62, 63
Duval, Isaac H., 145
Eagle, Henry, 20
Early, Jubal A., 101, 106, 107,
109, 115, 121-123, 134
Eastern Shore, 5
Easton, 44
Edward's Ferry, 24, 32, 46, 48,
76, 92, 130
Elder's Battery, 80, 81
Ellenborough, 153
Ellerbrock, Charles, 14
Ellicott Mills, 3, 119
Ely, Robert B., 27
Emancipation Proclamation, 64,
71, 98
Emmitsburg, 79, 133
Engles, William S., 30
Ent, William, 139
Erwin, John F., 68
Eshleman, B.F., 82, 83
Este, William F., 141
Evans, Clement, 118

Evett's Creek, 135
Fairchild, Harrison, 54
Fairfield, Pa., 84
Fairview Heights Signal Sation,
65
Falling Waters, 37, 90
Falls Run, 119
*Fanny,* 34
Farnsworth, John F., 48, 49, 51
Fay, John B., 144-146
Federal Hill, 19
Fields, Eugene, 127
Findlay, John V.L., 42
First Separate Brigade, 108
Fitzhugh, Thaddeus, 148
Fitzpatrick, Benjamin, 6
Fletcher, Capt., 23, 24
Flintstone Creek, 135
Flock's Mill, 135
Follansbee, A.S., 11, 12
Ford, Thomas H., 52
Fort Carroll, 13
Fort Delaware, De., 44
Fort DeRussy, 121
Fort Frederick, 38
Fort Lafayette, 44
Fort McHenry, 10, 13, 19-21, 44,
100
Fort Slocum, 122
Fort Stevens, 120-123, 130
Fort Sumter, S.C., 10, 25, 149
Fort Warren, Ma., 69
Fort Washington, 10
Fox, Watson A., 87
Fox's Gap, 55, 60
Franklin, William B., 60, 127-129
Frederick City, 3, 15, 16, 23, 29,
48, 50, 51, 54, 76, 103-106,
108, 119, 131, 137

Frederick County, 138
Freedman's Bureau, 141
Freedman's Rest, 141
French, William H., 79, 85
Frey, Edwin, 105, 120
Front Street Theater, 100
Frostburg, 24
Funkstown, 84, 86, 88
Furlong, R.W., 89
*G.W. Green,* 68
Garland, Samuel, 55, 60, 113
Garrett, John W., 3, 65, 107,
   152
Garrett, Richard, 152
Gassman, Jacob, 145, 146
Gatchell, William, 69
Geary, John W., 29, 30, 33
*George Washington Park Custis,*
   34
Gerrardsville, 120
Getty, George W., 35
Gilmor, Harry, 124, 125, 129,
   132
Gilpin, Charles, 104, 105
Gilpin, Gideon, 139
Glen Ellen, 127
Glenn, William W., 9
Glymont, 67
Godwin, Joseph M., 73
Goldsborough, Henry H., 99
Goldsmith, John M., 99
Gordon, John B., 118, 123
Gordon, J.P., 29
Govanstown, 129
Grant, Ulysses S., 98, 121, 135,
   138, 149
*Grapshot,* 67
Great Falls, 27, 28

Great Wicomico River, 19, 62,
   92
Green, Israel, 3
Green, Thomas, 129
Greenfields, Andrew J., 86
Green Spring Depot, W.V., 136
Green Spring Furnace, 66
Green Spring Valley, 125, 129
Grubb, Capt., 140
Gunpowder River, 12, 125, 128
*Habeas Corpus,* 19, 21, 72, 93
Hagers Mountain, 140
Hagerstown, 50, 54, 68, 80, 89,
   102, 132, 133, 137
Hall, Thomas W., 29, 69
Hallar, Ritchie, 144, 146
Halleck, Henry W., 121
Hampton, Wade, 51, 54
Hancock, 40, 41, 44, 132, 134,
   137
Hane, Samuel, 83
Harman, A.W., 73
Harpers Ferry, W.V., 1, 3, 17,
   23, 52, 53, 55, 85, 101, 107
*Harriet DeFord,* 148, 149
*Harriet Lane, U.S.S.,* 36
Harris, Benjamin G., 153
Harris, J. Morrison, 12
Harris, Thomas C., 128
Harris, William G., 69
Harrisburg, Pa., 102
Harrison Act. Mast., 37
Harrison Island, 32
Hart, J.F., 51
Hart's Battery, 82, 83
Hasbrouck, Henry C., 24
Hatcher, Harry, 133
Hauck Farm, 88
Haverstick, Capt., 129

Havre De Grace, 127, 128
Hawley, Joseph W., 87
Hayes, Capt., 80
Hayes, Peter, 99
Hayes, Rutherford B., 55, 145
Heath, Harry, 91
Henderson, John, 27
*Hercules,* U.S.R.V., 98
Herold, David, 150-152
Herriott, Vance, 144
Heter's Island, 31
Hicks, Thomas H., 9, 12, 13, 15, 16, 98, 110
Higgins, Patrick, 2
Hill, Daniel H., 46, 54, 55
Holland, T.R., 54
Hollins, George N., 26
Holmes, Oliver W., Jr., 123
Homans, Charles, 14
Hooker, Edward, 149
Hooker, Joseph, 43, 50, 62, 72
Horner, O.A., 103, 133
Howard, Gen., 12
Howard, Benjamin C., 33
Howard, Charles, 20, 69
Howard County, 57, 126
Howard, Frank K., 29, 69
Howard, O.O., 32, 86
Hulve, Peter, 79
Hunter, David, 106, 107, 127, 137-139
Illinois Military Units, 1st Art., 135; 8th Cav., 47-49, 51, 62, 66, 101, 102, 104, 106, 118, 120, 133, 134; 12th Cav., 65, 66
Imboden, John D., 75, 81, 83, 113
Independent Greys, 3

*Indiana,* 20
Indiana Military Units, 17th Art., 85, 86; 3rd Cav., 36, 47, 48, 51, 66; 11th Zouaves, 23; 12th Inf., 36; 20th Inf., 36; 27th Inf., 52
*Intrepid,* 34
*Isaac L. Adkins,* 99
*J.B. Spafford,* 148
*J.J. Houseman,* 93
Jackson, Thomas J., 23, 25, 40, 41, 49, 52, 62, 64
*Jacob Bell,* 31, 36, 67, 95
Jeff Davis Legion, 51
Jefferson, 48, 54
Jenkins, A.G., 74
Jodd, Henry B., 127, 128
Johnson, Andrew, 100, 141, 153
Johnson, Bradley T., 104, 106, 115, 122, 124, 125, 127, 129-132, 134, 136
Johnson, Cornelius, 73
Johnson, G.K., 119
Johnston, Joseph E., 39, 153
Jones Cross-Roads, 89
Jones, Edward F., 11, 58
Jones, Thomas A., 151, 152
Jones, William E., 73, 84
Jug Bridge, 108, 118
Kaig, John H., 2
Kane, George P., 12, 20, 25, 58, 69
Keedysville, 101, 137, 138
Keim, William H., 21
Kelly, B.F., 86, 135, 136, 144, 146
Kelly, T.W., 135
Kemp House, 88
Kemp, William H., 129

176

Kenly, John R., 25, 85, 112
Kennedy, Anthony, 12
Kennedy Farm, 2, 4, 56
Kilgore, Alexander, 94
Kilgore, Frank, 94
Kilpatrick, Judson, 80, 86, 90
King, Lt., 50
Knight, Capt., 50
Knight, N.B., 78
Knoxville, 85
Kuykendall, Joseph W., 145
Ladd & Whitney Monument,
    117, 154
Lakeman, Moses, 66
LaMountain, John, 34
Lancaster Greys, 19
Lander, F.W., 40
Latimar, T.W., 49
Laurel, 126, 131
Lawrence, W.L.J., 91
Leary, Peter, 104
Lee, Fitzhugh, 46, 47, 62, 84
Lee, G.W.C., 124
Lee, Robert E., 3, 39, 45, 47, 56,
    63-65, 134, 149, 154
Leitersburg, 80, 87
Leonardtown, 153
Leopole, Andrew, 100
Lewis, James, 127
Lightburn, Joseph A.J., 145
Limmerman, Capt., 133
Lincoln, Abraham, 6, 7, 10, 12,
    16, 19, 44, 45, 64, 65, 68, 72,
    93, 94, 100, 122, 123, 141,
    147, 149-152
Lincoln Hospital, 130
Little Georgetown, 132
Lockwood, Henry H., 34
Locust Point, 105

Logan, Thomas, 66
Lomax, L.L., 81
Longstreet, James, 40, 52, 54, 62
Loudon Rangers, See Mean's
    Ind. Cav.
Lowe, Thaddeus, S.C., 34
Lowell, Charles R., 129
Lower Marlboro, 32
Lumen, Theodore, 24
Lynn, Sprigg S., 146
Machodoc Creek, Va., 152
Maine Military Units, 3rd Inf.,
    66; 6th Inf., 89
Magnolia Station, 127
Magruder, William T., 24
*Malinda,* 100
Mansfield, Joseph K.F., 27
*Margaret,* 26
Marker, Caleb, 135
Marshal Kane Pike, 111
Marshall, Thomas, 84, 85
Martin, W.T., 51
Martinsburg, W.V., 3, 52, 107
*Mary Pierce,* 26
Maryland Club, 141
Maryland Heights, 33, 52, 53,
    85, 101, 107
Maryland Institute Hall, 9
Maryland Military Units,
    Maryland Guard, 12; CSA:
    Baltimore Light Artillery, 104,
    126, 130, 134-137; 1st Cav.,
    73, 125-127, 129, 132; 2nd
    Cav., 76, 126, 132; USA: 1st
    Artillery, 61, 109; 1st Cav., 47,
    48, 53, 65; Cole's Cavalry, 74,
    76, 85, 103, 132, 133, 137;
    Richard's Ind. Cav. Co., 34;
    1st Inf., 25, 38, 85; 4th Inf.,

85; 8th Inf., 85; 1st E.S. Inf., 34, 42, 77, 78; 1st Reg. P.H.B., 53; 2nd Reg. P.H.B., 30, 136; 3rd Reg. P.H.B., 104, 108; Purnell Legion, 34; Maryland Brigade, 85
Maryland Ore Bank, 30
Massachusetts Military Units, Cook's Battery, 18; 2nd Cav., 129; 5th Colored Cav., 139; 1st Inf., 28, 35; 6th Inf., 11, 18, 42; 8th Inf., 13
Mathias Point, 139
Mattawoman Creek, 34, 35
McCaffery, John, 84
McCausland, John, 102, 118, 134, 136
McClellan, George B., 39, 46, 50, 55, 60, 62, 63, 65, 68, 141
McCoy's Ferry, 87, 132
McCoy's Ford, 65
McCrea, E.P., 31
McDonald, Angus, 30
McDonald, E.H., 72
McElwee, George, 137
McGaw, Samuel, 41, 62, 67
McIntosh, John B., 88
McLaws, Lafayette, 52, 61
McLean, Hancock T., 102, 132
McNeill, Jesse, 145
McNeill's Rangers, 73, 144
McPhail, James L., 44
Meade, George G., 77
Mean's Ind. Cav., 75, 101, 103, 140
Meigs, Montgomery C., 120
Melvin, Thayer, 146
Merchants Exchange, 152
Merryman, John, 21, 72, 110, 125

Metz, Jacob A., 74
Michigan Military Units, 1st Cav., 90; 6th Cav., 74, 90
Middle Department, 43, 44, 92, 98, 104, 107, 138, 141
Middle Military Division, 138, 139
Miles, Dixon S., 53
Mill Creek, 19
Miller's Battery, 83
Millersville, 15
Milroy, Robert H., 75, 85
Monocacy Aquaduct, 46
Monocacy, battle of, 106, 120, 125, 138
Monocacy Bridge, 19, 48-50, 107
Monocacy Junction, 105, 108, 119
Monocacy River, 46, 66, 104, 106, 108, 119, 133
Monocacy Station, 3
Monrovia, 119
Montgomery County, 126
*Monticello, U.S.S.,* 20
Monument Square, 19, 45
Mooney, Robert, 133
Moor, August, 51
Moore's Battery, 83
Morris, William G., 93, 100
Mosby, John S., 74, 101, 120
Motkowski, Stanislaus, 128
Mountain House, 60
Mount Airy, 76
Mudd, Samuel A., 151, 152
Muddy Branch, 120
Munford, Thomas T., 47, 48, 54, 60, 61
Murdock, John, 49
Nanjemoy Creek, 27

Narcom, Capt., 83
National Road, 24, 50, 55, 60, 88, 89
National Union Party, 100
Nelson, 133
Nesbitt, A., 50
New Castle, De., 43
New Creek, W.V., 24
New Hampshire Military Units, 1st Inf., 23
New Market, 47, 118, 119
New Windsor, 125
New York Military Units, 3rd Art., 88; 5th Hv. Art., 46, 53; 8th Art., 19; 9th Art., 31; 5th Cav., 81; 9th Cav., 54; 11th Cav., 69; 16th Cav., 152; 21st Cav., 101, 103, 119; 7th Inf., 13, 15, 45; 8th Inf., 18; 9th Inf., 27, 29; 13th Inf., 19; 28th Inf., 65; 34th Inf., 31; 74th Inf., 87; 115th Inf., 53; 150th Inf., 78
Newport, R.I., 15
Nicherson, Sylvanas, 148
Nicholas, Wilson C., 126, 129
Noland's Ferry, 101, 130
Noland's Island, 31
Northampton County, Va., 34
North Carolina Military Units, 1st Cav., 86; 28th Inf., 91
North Central Railroad, 12, 125
Offuts Cross-Roads, 77
Ohio Military Units, 3rd Cav., 145; 28th Inf., 51; 32nd Inf., 52, 53; 87th Inf., 47; 109th Inf., 128; 143rd Inf., 136; 156th Inf., 135; 159th Inf., 104

Ohl, Martin, 27
O'Laughlin, Michael, 150
Old Town, 30, 135, 136
Ord, E.O.C., 120
Osborn, Francis C., 130
Owings Mills, 125
Owings, Nickolas, 129
Paine, Lewis, 151, 152
Painter's Mill, 125
Parker, Foxhall A., 98, 117
Patapsco River, 17
*Pawnee, U.S.S.,* 20, 22
Payne, A.D., 49
Payne, Nathaniel, 87
Pelham, John, 66
Pemberton, J.C., 10
Pendleton, George H., 141
Pendleton, William N., 63, 64
Pennington, J.B., 42
Pennington's Battery, 66, 67
Pennsylvania Military Units, Battery M, 37; 12th Cav., 87, 103, 133; 14th Cav., 137; 18th Cav., 80; 7th Pa. Res., 28; 17th Inf., 24; 25th Inf., 10; 28th Inf., 29-31, 33, 35, 37, 41; 29th Inf., 87; 96th Inf., 61
Perryville, 128
Peterson, William, 151
Petersville, 62
Petrie, Peter B., 136, 137
Pettigrew, James J., 113
Phelps, A.J., 2
Philadelphia City Scouts, 133
Philadelphia, Wilmington & Baltimore RR, 6, 125, 128
Philadelphia Zouaves D'Afrique, 69
Pierce, James A., 98

Pikesville, 129
Piney Point, 99
Piney Run Bridge, 77
Pleasant Valley, 52, 67, 85
Pleasonton, Alfred, 66
Point Lookout, 26, 29, 72, 91, 99, 107, 124, 126
Point of Rocks, 30, 37, 46, 47, 55, 74, 75, 100-102
Poolesville, 23, 46-48, 66, 68, 69, 120, 130
Pope, John, 40
Porter, Fitz-John, 64
Portsmouth Battery, 55
Port Tobacco, 139
Potomac Flotilla, 17, 21, 25, 26, 36, 41, 67, 98, 153
Potomac River, 17, 27, 37, 41, 43, 63, 81, 91, 93, 100; off Aquia Creek, 21; Cockpit Point, 40; Freestone Point, 31, 36; Jacks Creek, 66; Maryland Point, 67; Mathias Point, 25, 26, 33, 34; Millstone Landing, 36; Sewell's Point, 20, 22
Pratt, John S., 42
President Street Station, 11
Preston, A.W., 80
Price, Robert, 128
Prince Frederick County, 28
Prince Georges County, 16, 28, 32, 149
Prince William Cavalry, 74
Pritchards Mill, see Antietam Ford
Quesenberry, Mrs., 152
*R.R. Coyler, U.S.S.,* 15
Ramseur, S.D., 109
Rastall, John E., 42, 43

Rathbone, Henry, 150
Read, Capt., 53
Read, William, 153
Relay, 3, 17, 18, 65, 152
*Reliance, U.S.S.,* 37
Reno, Jesse, 50, 60, 113
*Resolute, U.S.S.,* 22, 67
Revere House, 145, 146
Rhode Island Military Units, 1st Art., 88
Rich Hill, 151
Richards, A.E., 102
Richards, Capt., 34
Richmond, Nathaniel, 80
Rickett, James B., 108, 118
Rickett's Run, 139
Riggs, George, 27
Ringgold Battery, 78
Rivers' House, 122
*Robert Knowles,* 93
Roberts, James D., 30
Roberts, Scott W., 32
Robinson, J.C., 14
Robinson, John F.D., 92
Rockville, 22, 76-94, 110-121, 129, 139
Rode, Robert, 60, 109
Rodgers, George W., 13, 15
Rodman, Isaac P., 54
Rose Hill, 23
Rosser, Thomas, 55
Rowley, W.W., 65
Run Point, 38
Rush's Lancers, 54
Russell, Charles H., 47, 48, 65
St. George Island, 95
St. James College, 83
St. Jerome's Creek, 68
St. Johns College, 144

*St. Mary's,* 148
*St. Mary's Beacon,* 72
Saint Marys County, 32, 149, 151, 153
St. Mary's, port of, 148
*St. Nicholas,* 26
Salem Zouaves, 13
Salisbury, 42
Sammon, Col., 53
*Samuel Pearsall,* 93
Sanders, William P., 50
Sandy Hook, 2, 3, 27, 41, 100, 101, 105
Sandy Springs, 139
*Satellite, U.S.S.,* 41, 92
Schaumbery, Capt., 50
Schenck, Robert, 92, 94
Schulze, Gerhard C., 95
Schurz, Carl, 86
Scott, T. Parkin, 69
Scott, Winfield, 17, 19, 25
Scott's 900, 92, 94, 99
Secret Line, 149, 150
*Seminole, U.S.S.,* 31
Seneca, 31
Seneca Mills, 23, 74
Severn River, 18
Seward, William H., 151
Sharpsburg, 76
Shenandoah Valley, 101, 106, 107, 130
Shepard, S.G., 90
Sheppard, Hayward, 2, 3
Sheridan, Philip, 67
Sheridan, Philip H., 97, 138, 139
Sickles, Daniel E., 34
Silver Springs, 121, 123, 126
Simpson, J.L., 135
Slocum, Henry, 60

Smallwood Infantry, 32
Smith Point Lighthouse, 19
Smith, William F., 61
Smith, William P., 3
Smithsburg, 79
Smithville, 28
Smryna, De., 43
Soloman's Gap, 52, 53, 86, 101, 104
Somerset County, 114
*The South,* 29, 69
South Carolina Military Units, 2nd Cav., 51
South Mountain, 52, 54, 55, 61, 86, 138
South River Expedition, 130
Southern Maryland, 5, 28, 32, 107, 122, 125, 149-151
Spangler, Edman, 150
Stanton, Edwin M., 69
Stanton, George, 144
Steiner, John A., 53
Steuart, George H., 3
Stirling, Thomas H., 128
Stone, Charles P., 30
Stonebreaker's Barn, 88
Stoneman, George, 69
Stough, Israel, 136
Stover's Woods, 88
Stuart, J.E.B., 3, 4, 48, 55, 60, 64, 79, 86
Stuart Horse Artillery, 55
Sugar Loaf Mountain, 48, 50
Surratt, John, 150
Surratt, Mary, 149, 151, 152
Surrattsville, 150, 151
Susquehanna River, 13, 17, 128
Swan, Oswald, 151
Swann, Thomas, 141, 144

Sykesville, 73
T.B., 151
Talbot County, 99
*Tallahassee, C.S.S.,* 124
Taney, Roger B., 21, 110
*Teaser, U.S.S.,* 67
Tennessee Military Units, 1st
    Inf., 90
The Caves, 125
Thomas, Al, 139
Thomas' Farm, 109, 138
*Thomas Freeborn,* 20, 22, 25,
    26, 62, 67, 93
Thomas, Capt., 19
Thomas, Richard, 26
Thorpe, Major, 103
*Three Brothers,* 92
Tibbs, T.A., 54
Tidball's Battery, 62, 83, 88
Tole, James C., 67
Toucey, Isaac, 10
Towsontown, 128, 129
Triadelphia, 126
Trimble, Isaac R., 13
Turner Rifles, 27
Turner's Gap, 52, 55, 60, 118
Tyler, Erastus B., 105, 106, 108
Union Home Guard, 24
Unseld, John, 3
Upper Marlboro, 28
Urbana, 47, 51, 106, 118, 119
U.S. Military Organizations, 2nd
    Art., 48; 3rd Art., 51, 79; 5th
    Art., 24, 25; 1st Cav., 85; 6th
    Cav., 50, 84, 102, 132; 2nd
    U.S. Colored Cav., 100; 5th
    Inf., 14; Marines, 3, 4, 10;
    Naval Academy, 13, 15;
    Signal Corps, 47

*Valley City, U.S.S.,* 31
Vandiver, George, 145, 146
Vermont Brigade, 88, 89
Vermont Military Units, 1st
    Cav., 81; 10th Inf., 109
Vernon, George W., 76
Veteran Reserve Corps, 127
*Vicksburg, U.S.S.,* 130
*Victory,* 36
Virginia Military Units, 1st Cav.,
    49, 50; 4th Cav., 77; 7th Cav.,
    48, 79, 84, 145, 146; 8th Cav.,
    136; 9th Cav., 50, 62, 77, 80,
    81; 10th Cav., 65, 80; 11th
    Cav., 72, 145; 12th Cav., 47,
    48, 73, 89; 17th Cav., 119;
    27th Bat., 136; 35th Bat., 69,
    75, 92; 43rd Bat., 74, 101,
    133, 139; 2nd Inf., 30, 37;
    40th Inf., 25
Wachapreague Inlet, 93
Waid, C.F., 67
Waite, John M., 153
Wauldhauer, David, 51
Walker, Elijah, 66
Walker, John S., 22
Wallace, James, 42
Wallace, Lew, 23, 98, 104-108,
    115, 118, 141
Waller, Capt., 47, 50
Wallis, Severn T., 69
Wampler, George E., 32
Ward, James H., 17, 20, 22, 25,
    26
*Ward, T.A., U.S.S.,* 68
Warfield, Henry M., 69
Washington Artillery of New
    Orleans, 82, 83

Washington Artillery of Potts-
 ville, Pa., 11
Washington County, 100
Washington, D.C., 3, 15, 16,
 26, 107, 118, 119, 121-124,
 126
Washington, Naval Yard, 10, 21,
 22, 26, 34, 150
Washington, Richard, 81
Weber, Max, 101
Weber, Peter A., 90, 91
Webring, Samuel, 68
Wellersburg, 24
Wells, Major, 118, 120
Wells, Gideon, 17, 119, 153
Welton, Isaac S., 145
West, J.B., 121
West Virginia Military Units, 1st
 Cav., 80, 137; 10th Cav., 133;
 6th Inf., 73, 135; 1st Inf., 145;
 11th Inf., 135
Western Maryland, 5, 45, 79,
135
Western Maryland Railroad, 125
Westminster, 31, 77, 78, 125
White, Col., 88
White, E.V., 69, 74, 92
White's Ford, 67, 130, 140

Whitescarver, George H., 74
Whittier, John T., 53
Wigfall, Louis T., 31
Wiley's Ford, 146
*William Woodward,* 19
Williams, Lt., 50
Williams, William, 2
Williamsport, 25, 41, 64, 74,
 81-83, 90, 131, 132, 137
Wilmington, De., 43
Winans Ross, 18
Winans' Steam Gun, 111
Wise, Henry, 3
Wise, Joseph, 42
Wofford, William T., 84
Wood, John T., 124
Woodstock, 126
Wool, John E., 44, 45
Worthington's Farm, 109
Wright, Horatio G., 89, 121, 122
*Wyandank, U.S.S.,* 148
Wyman, R.H., 36, 41
Wynkoop, George C., 13
Young, P.M.B., 54
Zachiah Swamp, 151
Zarvona's Zouaves, 26
Zimmerman, 138